GRIDS

GRIDS

Creative Solutions
for Graphic Designers

wiley.com

Published by John Wiley & Sons, Inc., Hoboken, New Jersey
Published simultaneously in Canada

For general information about our other products and services, please contact our
Customer Care Department within the United States at (800) 762-2974, outside the
United States at (317) 572-3993 or fax (317) 572-4002.

Wiley also publishes its books in a variety of electronic formats. Some content that
appears in print may not be available in electronic books. For more information about
Wiley products, visit our web site at www.wiley.com.

Library of Congress Cataloging-in-Publication Data

Roberts, Lucienne.
  Grids : creative solutions for graphic designers / by Lucienne Roberts.
    p. cm.
  Includes index.
  ISBN 978-0-470-19508-6 (pbk.)
  1. Grids (Typographic design) 2. Graphic arts. 3. Commercial art. I. Title.
  NC998.4.R57 2008
  686.2'24--dc22
                        2007043777

Reprographics in Singapore by ProVision Pte. Ltd.
Tel: +65 6334 7720
Fax: +65 6334 7721

Printed in China by Midas Printing International Ltd.

10 9 8 7 6 5 4 3 2 1

The CD and tutorials

The grids featured in this book are included on the accompanying CD, and have been recreated in both InDesign and QuarkXPress. To locate the grid you wish to utilize in either of these applications, simply look for the file name that matches the page number on which the grid appears in the book.

In addition to this useful resource, a series of tutorials that introduce readers to the process of grid design have been created exclusively for this book, and are available to download using the following URL:

www.wiley.com/college/roberts

Measurements

All measurements have been given in millimeters or points. If you prefer working in inches, most applications provide this option in the measurements palette.

Contents

Introduction 008

Catalogs, leaflets & brochures 020

Exhibitions 036

Illustrated books 058

Identities 096

Magazines, newspapers & newsletters 118

Packaging 170

Posters & fliers 188

Index 222

Introduction

This whole business of grids is so difficult for graphic designers. Most of us love them. But we're scared of revealing any nerdy or, worse still, despotic tendencies so we jump nervously from foot to foot, simultaneously belittling and venerating the grid. We've got to appear to be casual about it—but not so much so that our peers think we're grid lightweights.

The problem is partly one of association. A grid is generally a series of straight vertical and horizontal lines so, if you're interested in grids are you "straight" in other ways too? This book sets out to demonstrate that, ultimately, it's not the notion of the grid that is important—it's the hand that constructs, the brain that computes, and the perspicacious eye that exploits these invisible structures.

A graphic-design grid is a bit like magic (now you see it, now you don't) sets of intersecting lines that help the designer decide where to put things, but that generally no one else sees. The benefits of using a grid are multifarious, ranging from the psychological to the functional, and, of course, the aesthetic. The grid embodies all the contradictions that designers struggle with. This is the designer's very own enigma code that can elevate design discourse to that of a science, and eradicate the creative block by "virtually" filling the blank page.

What is a grid?

A grid subdivides a page vertically and horizontally into margins, columns, inter-column spaces, lines of type, and spaces between blocks of type and images. These subdivisions form the basis of a modular and systematic approach to the layout, particularly for multipage documents, making the design process quicker, and ensuring visual consistency between related pages.

At its most basic, the sizes of a grid's component parts are determined by ease of reading and handling. From the sizes of type to the overall page or sheet size, decision-making is derived from physiology and the psychology of perception as much as by aesthetics. Type sizes are generally determined by hierarchy—captions smaller than body text and so on—column widths by optimum word counts of eight to ten words to the line, and overall layout by the need to group related items. This all sounds rather formulaic, and easy. But designers

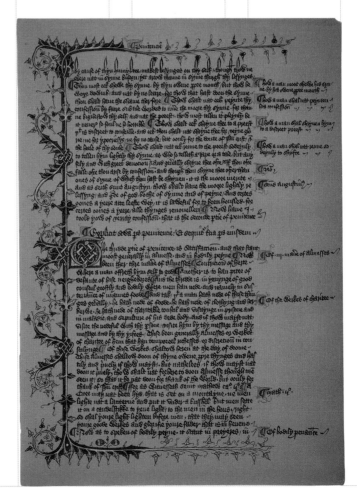

Left
This facsimile page is from a fourteenth-century English manuscript. The overall layout is asymmetric, and therefore surprisingly modern. The main column is positioned to the left of the page, with a large right-hand margin used for notes. All text is calligraphic and ranged left.

The first five hundred years

Philosophers and linguists have argued that nothing exists in our consciousness unless it is named and we have a language with which to discuss it. Neither "graphic design" nor "grids" were talked about until the mid-twentieth century. Once named, complex grid structures comprising multiple columns, fields, baseline grids, and so on poured forth as never before, but it's not true to say that designers or their predecessors—commercial artists, printers, and scribes—hadn't been thinking about content, proportion, space, and form before this.

Even prior to typesetting and printing there were texts available to read. These were religious texts laid out by scribes in calligraphy. The pages were surprisingly modern, often using more than one column, with lettering that was ranged left, and color and variations in letter size used for emphasis. Just as the first cars resembled a horse-drawn carriage, the first printed

pages took their cue from the manuscript page. But over time one major difference was introduced—justified setting. In this, spaces between words in continuous text are adjusted in each line so that columns align on both left and right sides. Although manuscript pages were symmetrical when viewed as spreads, the ranged-left lettering made them essentially asymmetric. With justified setting came 450 years of symmetry, and it wasn't until the twentieth century that this convention was truly challenged.

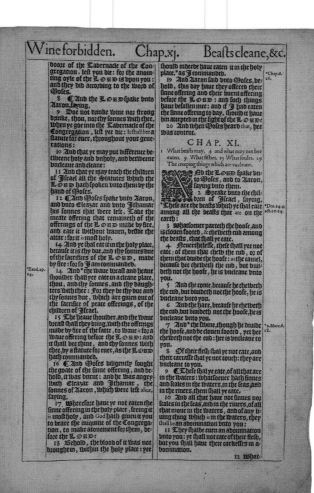

Left
Although derived from calligraphic forms, this lettering is actually type. Taken from a late-sixteenth-century English Bible, this page shows how printers quickly adopted symmetry. The text is justified and the two columns placed symmetrically on the page, with hanging notes also positioned according to a central axis.

Proportion and geometry

From the beginnings of printing (from the mid-fifteenth century) until the Industrial Revolution (late eighteenth century), the book was the primary output of printing. Apart from verse, type was generally set in one justified column per page, placed symmetrically on the spread with larger outer margins than inner, and a larger margin at the foot than at the head. But just as each decision made in minimal art is hugely significant, so too were the relative relationships of these few elements on the page. The proportions of these pages and margins were determined by geometry, concerned with the relation of points, lines, surfaces, and solids to one another rather than their measurement.

There are many geometrical constructions that can produce a beautiful page, but the golden section is usually cited as the most successful. As it is a geometrically derived form, it can be drawn with a setsquare and a compass—no measuring required. For those who do like to know measurements, the relationship of short to long side of a golden rectangle is 1:1.618. Many contemporary designers find this apparently irregular ratio unsettlingly chaotic, but others feel that the number sequence at its core has almost magical properties. By adding the lengths of the long and short edges it is possible to arrive at the next measurement in the sequence to give a bigger rectangle of the same proportions. This also works in reverse in order to make a smaller rectangle.

Adding two numbers to find the next in a series is also the basis of the number progression of the Fibonacci sequence, named after the thirteenth-century Italian mathematician who first identified it in many natural forms, from the arrangements of petals to the spirals of seashells. A combination of the golden section and Fibonacci sequence (1, 1, 2, 3, 5, 8, 13, etc) was often used to determine the overall proportion of the page and margins of the classical book.

Left

This diagram shows how to draw a golden-section rectangle using only a set square and a compass. The resulting proportions are considered to be some of the most aesthetically pleasing. Start by using a set square to draw a right angle. Place a compass in one corner and draw an arc to arrive at a square, then draw a line horizontally through its center. Use the compass to join the two points shown to complete the rectangle.

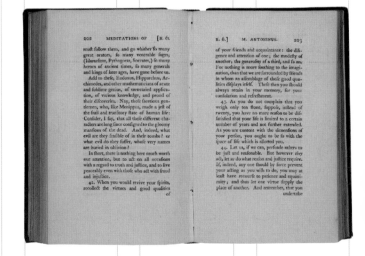

Above

This spread from The Meditations of Marcus Aurelius Antoninus, *published in 1792, uses the golden section to determine the text area, and the Fibonacci sequence to arrive at relative margin sizes (inner margin 3 units; top and outer margins 5 units; bottom margin 8 units). The gutter is treated as the central axis, and there is one column of text. The outer and bottom margins are larger than the inner and top. These optical adjustments ensure that the text doesn't appear to be falling off the bottom of the page.*

The next hundred years

The Industrial Revolution marked the beginning of a capital-based economy, with mass production at its heart. Graphic design was born, although still not named as such. Its job was to communicate diverse messages to an increasingly literate people. The rise in print output was phenomenal—posters, leaflets, and advertising of all kinds, newspapers, timetables, and all manner of information-based design. Suddenly designs competed for attention. Images, initially in the form of engravings and then as photographs, had to be incorporated along with an ever-expanding array of display typefaces. Highly skilled and educated printers stayed firmly in the land of the book, while jobbing printers and compositors struggled to lay out this diverse material for which the classical book was not a useful precedent.

Toward the end of the nineteenth century, artists and thinkers identified this as a problem that had to be solved. Although the work produced by William Morris and the Arts and Crafts movement may appear very different from that of modernism, Arts and Crafts was its forerunner in one important respect. Morris believed that form and function were inextricably entwined. Running almost concurrently with these ideas were the revolutionary cubist experiments of Picasso and Braque,

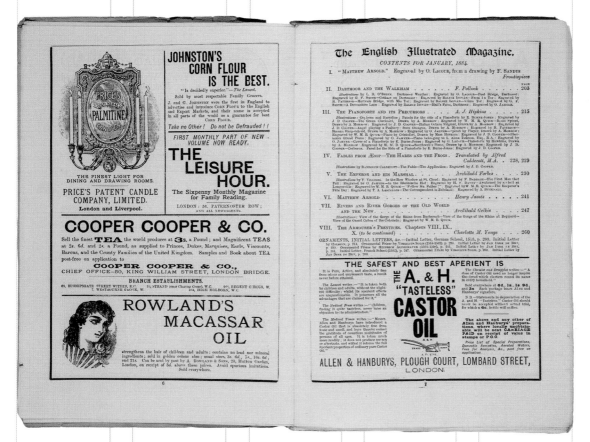

who were exploring how to represent 3-D forms on 2-D planes, producing increasingly abstract results. Artists, and then designers, were influenced by this work, and re-evaluated composition as a result.

The early twentieth-century art movements—futurism, dadaism, surrealism, constructivism, suprematism, and expressionism—also had an influence on the development of the grid. Artists were united in trying to represent a new, industrialised age exemplified by speed of travel and faster communication. They recognized the power of the word and broke with all previous print tradition by using type at conflicting angles or on curves; introducing extreme variation in type sizes; using drawn, abstracted letterforms; and generally ignoring the vertical and horizontal nature of type. For the first time, space was used as a dynamic component in typographic layout. The ethos that underpins this work was the antithesis of the rational and logical approach implicit in the grid. But in drawing such a resolute line under the past, it opened the door to de Stijl, the Bauhaus, and typographers like Herbert Bayer and Jan Tschichold, who called for some order to be imposed on what seemed like fractured chaos.

Above

This page is from an issue of the Futurist magazine Lacerba, *published in 1914. By breaking with previous approaches to layout and design, early twentieth-century art movements had an influence on the development of the grid. The work was often intentionally chaotic, but as the old rules were broken, a new, more rational system was given the space to develop.*

de Stijl, the Bauhaus, and Jan Tschichold

In 1917 Dutch architect, designer, and painter Theo van Doesburg founded de Stijl. The importance of this movement to the grid is that it explored form as determined by function, and placed this in a political context. Arguing that simplicity of form was accessible and democratic, its members advocated minimalism, using only rectilinear forms, and eradicating surface decoration other than as a byproduct of a limited color palette: the primaries plus black and white. The typographers affiliated to de Stijl wanted to apply these ideas in the real world, not just for their artistic cause. Designers like Piet Zwart and Paul Schuitema used these principles to produce commercial advertising and publicity materials.

The Bauhaus opened its doors in Weimar, Germany, in 1919, with the architect Walter Gropius as its Director. His belief that architecture, graphic art, industrial design, painting, sculpture, and so on were all interrelated had a profound impact on the development of typography and graphic design long after the school was forced to close by the Nazis in the 1930s. Within an astonishingly short period of time, graphic artists were marrying analytical skills with abstract form to arrive at mass-produced designs determined as much by political idealism as by a desire for self-expression. In 1925, Herbert Bayer was appointed to run the new printing and advertising work-shop. He paid attention to typographic detail, experimenting with a limited typo-graphic palette in order to achieve greater visual clarity and easily navigable pages.

During the late 1920s and the 1930s, typographer Jan Tschichold set out his typographic principles in two seminal books: *The New Typography* (1928), and *Asymmetric Typography* (1935). Tschichold's work was more refined than much of that which had preceded it. He wrote of typographic consistency as a necessary precursor to understanding, described designers as akin to engineers, and argued compellingly for asymmetry as a central tenet of modernism. It was the logical way to lay out text that is read from left to right, and produced "natural" rather than "formalist" solutions to the new design challenges than classicism, with its enforced central axis. In his work Tschichold explored subtle horizontal and vertical alignments, and used a limited range of fonts, type sizes, and type weights.

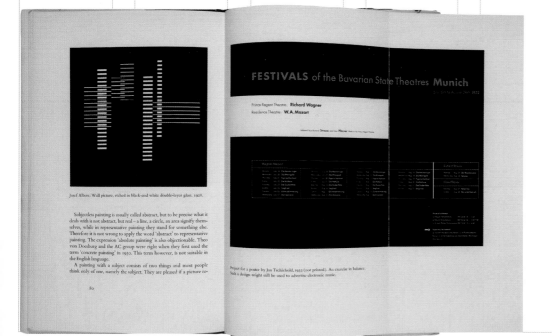

Josef Albers: Wall picture, etched in black-and-white double-layer glass. 1928.

Subjectless painting is usually called abstract, but to be precise what it deals with is not abstract, but real – a line, a circle, an area signify themselves, while in representative painting they stand for something else. Therefore it is not wrong to apply the word 'abstract' to representative painting. The expression 'absolute painting' is also objectionable. Theo von Doesburg and the AC group were right when they first used the term 'concrete painting' in 1930. This term however, is not suitable in the English language.

A painting with a subject consists of two things and most people think only of one, namely the subject. They are pleased if a picture re-

80

FESTIVALS of the Bavarian State Theatres Munich

Prince Regent Theatre: **Richard Wagner**
Residence Theatre: **W.A. Mozart**

Project for a poster by Jan Tschichold, 1932 (not printed). An exercise in balance. Such a design might still be used to advertise electronic music.

The grid and Swiss typography

Early modernists had explored layout, space, and scale. They had talked of the democratizing benefits of mass production, and had used the language of science as much as art. They had argued for consistency and minimalism as a mark of design confidence and greater accessibility. During WWII, and in the decades that followed, these ideas coalesced into a coherent design manifesto with a new design device at its core—the grid.

The grid and Swiss typography are synonymous. Switzerland was neutral during the war. Not only did it attract many intellectual refugees, including designers like Jan Tschichold, but also most

peacetime activities continued as normal, and supplies of such things as ink and paper weren't rationed. Added to this, publications had to be set in its three official languages—French, German, and Italian—which called for a modular approach, using multiple column structures.

Several Swiss artist/designers, most notably Max Bill and Richard Paul Lohse, explored systematic forms in their paintings concurrently with graphic design, while the graphic designers Emil Ruder and Josef Müller-Brockmann both wrote educative texts explaining what grids were and how to use them. They approached the subject with great rigor, arguing passionately that "integral design" required structures that would unite all the elements in both 2-D and 3-D design: type, pictures, diagrams, and space itself. Despite their enthusiasm

for order and precision, they both understood the value of artistic intuition.

"No system of ratios, however ingenious, can relieve the typographer of deciding how one value should be related to another... He must spare no effort to tutor his feeling for proportion... He must know intuitively when the tension between several things is so great that harmony is endangered. But he must also know how to avoid relationships lacking in tension since these lead to monotony." **Emil Ruder**, *Typography*

The grid and the design philosophy of which it is a part have been criticized for placing the narcissistic designer at the heart of the solution, and generating formulaic solutions that are mechanistic, unyielding, and rigid. But for Ruder, Müller-Brockmann, and many other designers since, the grid was the natural response to a design problem. It was also a metaphor for the human condition, and was found in all areas of human endeavor.

"Just as in nature, systems of order govern the growth and structure of animate and inanimate matter, so human activity itself has, since the earliest times, been distinguished by the quest for order... The desire to bring order to the bewildering confusion of appearances reflects a deep human need." **Josef Müller-Brockmann**, *Grid Systems in Graphic Design*

Right

The ingenuity of the "A" paper sizing system appeals to designers who are interested in modular approaches to design. For the true modernist, working with standard paper sizing is more economic and celebrates mass production. But, for designers who want to usurp the system, there are countless ways to subdivide the sheet sizes to arrive at more unusual formats.

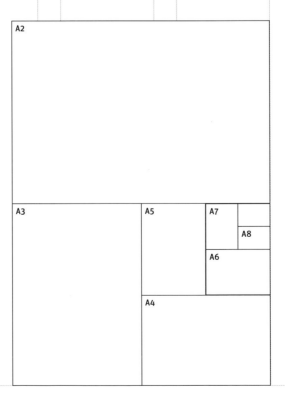

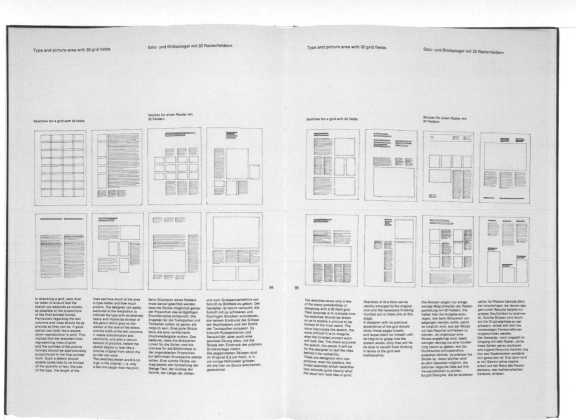

Sketches for a grid with 32 fields   Skizzen für einen Raster mit 32 Feldern   Sketches for a grid with 32 fields   Skizzen für einen Raster mit 32 Feldern

94   95

In sketching a grid, care must be taken to ensure that the sketch corresponds as closely as possible to the proportions of the final printed format. Particulars regarding the text columns and lines should be as precise as they can be. A good sketch can look like a scaled-down reproduction in print. This implies that the sketched lines representing lines of print and the outlines of the picture formats should be approximately proportional to the final printed work. Such a sketch should enable some idea to be formed of the quantity of text, the size of the type, the length of the lines and how much of the area is type matter and how much picture. The designer can easily succumb to the temptation to indicate the type with excessively heavy and imprecise strokes of the pencil which give no intimation of the size of the letters and the width of the text columns. It needs concentration and sensibility, and also a certain amount of practice, before the sketch begins to look like a precise original from which the printer can work.
The sketches shown are 6.5 cm high in the original, i. e. only a few mm larger than the print.

Beim Skizzieren eines Rasters muss darauf geachtet werden, dass die Skizze möglichst genau der Proportion des endgültigen Druckformates entspricht. Die Angaben für die Textspalten und Textzeilen sollen so genau als möglich sein. Eine gute Skizze kann wie eine verkleinerte Druckwiedergabe wirken. Das bedeutet, dass die skizzierten Linien für die Zeilen und die Umrisse für die Bildformate in der angenäherten Proportion zur definitiven Drucksache stehen sollen. Eine solche Skizze vermag bereits die Vorstellung der Menge Text, der Grösse der Schrift, der Länge der Zeilen und vom Grössenverhältnis von Schrift zu Bildfeld zu geben. Der Gestalter ist leicht versucht, die Schrift mit zu schweren und flüchtigen Strichen anzudeuten, die keinen Eindruck der Grösse der Buchstaben und der Breite der Textspalten zulassen. Es braucht Konzentration und Sensibilität, aber auch eine gewisse Übung dazu, bis die Skizze den Eindruck der präzisen Druckvorlage liefert.
Die abgebildeten Skizzen sind im Original 6,5 cm hoch, d. h. als sie hier im Druck erscheinen, gezeichnet.

The sketches show only a few of the many possibilities of designing with a 32-field grid. Their purpose is to indicate how the sketches should be drawn so as to enable a picture to be formed of the final result. The more inaccurate the sketch, the more difficult it is to imagine what the finished printed work will look like. The more accurate the sketch, the easier it will be for the designer to test the idea behind it for suitability.
There are designers who can produce, even for posters, the tiniest sketches which nevertheless intimate quite clearly what the result will look like in print.

Sketches of this kind can be readily enlarged to the original size and the necessary finishing touches put to them only at this stage.
A designer with no previous experience of the grid should study these pages closely and experiment for himself until he begins to grasp how the system works. Only then will he be able to benefit from thinking in terms of the grid and mathematics.

Die Skizzen zeigen nur einige wenige Möglichkeiten der Rastergestaltung mit 32 Feldern. Sie haben hier die Aufgabe anzuregen, wie beim Skizzieren vorgegangen werden sollte, damit so möglich wird, aus der Skizze auf das Resultat schliessen zu können. Je ungenauer eine Skizze angefertigt wird, desto weniger vermag sie eine Vorstellung davon zu geben, wie die Drucksache schliesslich aussehen könnte. Je präziser die Skizze ist, desto leichter wird es dem Gestalter möglich, die dahinter liegende Idee auf ihre Verwendbarkeit zu prüfen.
Es gibt Designer, die es verstehen, selbst für Plakate kleinste Skizzen anzufertigen, bei denen das gedruckte Resultat bereits mit grosser Deutlichkeit zu erahnen ist. Solche Skizzen sind leicht auf die Originalgrösse zu vergrössern, wobei erst dort die notwendigen Feinkorrekturen vorgenommen werden.
Der Gestalter, noch ungeübt im Umgang mit dem Raster, sollte diese Seiten genau studieren und eigene Versuche machen, bis ihm das Rastersystem verständlich geworden ist. Erst dann wird er mit Gewinn seine eigene Arbeit auf der Basis des Rasterdenkens, des mathematischen Denkens, erleben.

Left

Several post-War Swiss designers are the best-known exponents of the grid. This spread is from Josef Müller-Brockmann's Grid Systems in Graphic Design, *in which he explains, in meticulous detail, how multicolumn and field-based grids can be used flexibly to achieve any number of different layouts, in both 2-D and 3-D work.*

Below

This spread and throw-out from Anthony Froshaug's Typographic Norms, *published in 1964, explores the modular measurement systems that were at the heart of typography and letterpress printing at the time, and which are the basis of many grid structures today.*

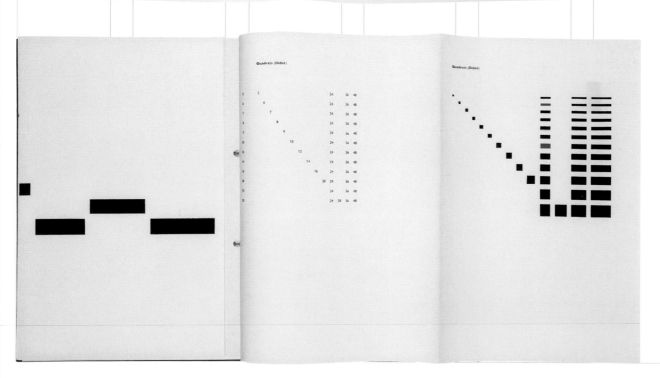

Quadrats (Didot)   Quadrats (Didot)

Grids and mathematics

The difference between grids as we know them and the page layouts of the past rests in increased flexibility and mathematical dexterity. This starts with considering format and ends with baseline grids, for which lines are often subdivided into units as small as 2pt. The computer has made greater precision easy, and contemporary grids subdivide the page into small component parts that can be combined in numerous ways that still ensure cohesion in the design. Small columns are joined to make wider columns, numbers of baseline units are joined to make fields, and so on.

Karl Gerstner's grid for the journal *Capital*, designed in 1962, is still often cited as near-perfect in terms of its mathematical ingenuity. The smallest unit in Gerstner's grid, or matrix as he called it, is 10pt—the baseline to baseline measurement of the text. The main area for text and images is a square, with an area above for titles and running heads. The cleverness lies in the subdivision of the square into 58 equal units in both directions. If all intercolumn spaces are two units, then a two-, three-, four-, five-, or six-column structure is possible without any leftover units.

The grid made visible

Grids are generally made visible only through use, but some designers have exposed the workings of the graphic design machine to demonstrate that the grid is something not only of utility, but also of beauty. Once visible, the precision of the grid acts as evidence of design credibility, and its purity of form has a mystical draw.

The Dutch designer Wim Crouwel pioneered the application of systematic design in the Netherlands during the 1950s and 1960s. His identity for the Vormgevers exhibition at the Stedelijk Museum in Amsterdam in 1968 used an exposed grid in the layout of posters and catalogs, which was also the basis of the lettering. In 1990, issue 7 of 8vo's influential journal *Octavo* ran grids with coordinates, like maps, under

Above
The Swiss designer Karl Gerstner's 1962 grid for the periodical Capital *is near perfect. His unit, both horizontally and vertically, was 10pt—the baseline to baseline measurement of the text type. The type area was a square of 58 units. Allowing for intercolumn spaces, this gave Gerstner grids of two, three, four, five, and six columns and fields.*

Right
Dutch designer Wim Crouwel is known for his exploration and experimentation with grids. In this poster for the Vormgevers exhibition in 1968, he made the grid visible. This device then formed the basis not only for the layout, but also for the lettering.

each spread. *Octavo* called their method of working "visual engineering."

"To get things built, you have to be able to describe them... The act of specifying requires one to define the structure of a design very precisely... It places one's design under intense scrutiny in terms of structure and logical process. Very different to the 'drag and drop' computer screen environment, where close enough is often good enough." **Mark Holt and Hamish Muir**, *8vo: On the Outside*

Designer Astrid Stavro has taken this one stage further. Inspired by a diverse set of grids, from the Gutenberg Bible to the *Guardian* newspaper, Stavro's GRID-IT notepads celebrate the usually invisible graphic-design grid in its purist form—unused and unsullied. Perhaps we can take this as a sign that designers no longer worry about being a little nerdy or despotic.

Left

Having started the journal Octavo, designers 8vo edited and designed it from the mid 1980s to the early 1990s. The design often explored systematic and modular approaches, but in issue 7 the designers chose to reveal their methods by giving the grid coordinates, like a map, and printing it as a background to each page.

Above

Italian designer Astrid Stavro worked on the Grid-it! Notepads project while studying at London's Royal College of Art. The intention is to celebrate the notion of the grid in its pure form. Each pad shows a different grid. These range from Tschichold and Müller-Brockmann classics to the Gutenberg Bible and Guardian newspaper. [Photographer: Mauricio Salinas]

Catalogs, leaflets & brochures

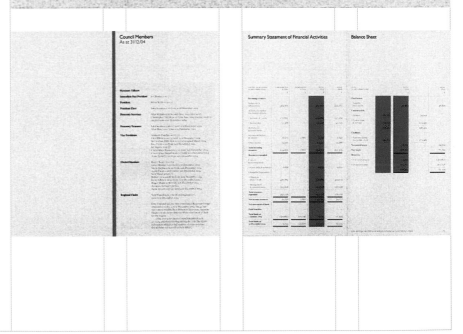

Grids: Creative Solutions for Graphic Designers

Below The voice of the
Society—our magazine,
The Designer issues 23 to 24

CSD ANNUAL REVIEW 2004
Design: Brad Yendle at Design Typography

Design Typography found inspiration
for this 24-page annual review in Karel
Marten's SUNschrift book covers from
the 1970s and 1980s. Marten's covers
are printed in two colors, creating a third
color through overprinting. They say that
necessity is the mother of invention—
designer Brad Yendle introduced this
technique here not only to make visible
the structure of the page, but also to
enliven some of the inconsistent and
undistinguished photography that had
been supplied. Yendle describes his grid
as fairly standard—four columns with
a deeper-than-average top margin—but
by introducing the offset colored blocks,
he has simultaneously broken the grid
and reinforced the clarity of his design.

GRID SPECIFICATIONS

Page size (trimmed)	150 x 297mm
Top margin	7mm
Bottom margin	15mm
Outside margin	7mm
Inside margin	7mm
Number of columns	4
Gutter width	4mm
Extras	Baseline grid, 12pt starting at 87.2mm

ISLINGTON

Islington has long been known as one of London's most fashionable and stylish boroughs. It draws its vibrant character from around the world and there is a real sense of community in this thriving and prosperous area. Home to some of the most diverse shopping in London, it offers unrivalled choice.

Crafted by CARROT.

L'ÉCOLE

Available January 2007

CARROT

L'ÉCOLE

L'École, a former Victorian schoolhouse and architectural landmark, located on the northern fringes of Islington, has been crafted into 52 spacious apartments by Carrot. L'École consists of two buildings, a sympathetic conversion of the Victorian schoolhouse and a contemporary new building. The two buildings sit side by side, designed in unison and working together to create a distinctive development where 21st-century technology is mixed with classic Victorian elegance. The development embodies Carrot's philosophy of creating individually crafted spaces with a modern style, whilst retaining a warm, sensuous feel.

ISLINGTON Islington has long been known as one of London's most fashionable and stylish boroughs. It draws its vibrant character from around the world and there is a real sense of community in this thriving and prosperous area. Home to some of the most diverse shopping in London, it offers unrivalled choice.

GRID SPECIFICATIONS

Page size (trimmed)	330 x 310mm
Top margin	25mm
Bottom margin	18mm
Outside margin	25mm
Inside margin	15mm
Number of columns	8
Gutter width	5mm
Extras	Baseline grid, 21.5pt starting at 35.7mm

L'ÉCOLE PROPERTY BROCHURE

Design: Brad Yendle at Design Typography

L'École, a former school in north London, was redeveloped by Carrot into a variety of apartments. The building took shape in several phases, so designers Brad Yendle and Zoë Bather were briefed to develop a flexible system that could be updated and added to easily over time. This requirement informed all aspects of the design. The publication is loose-leaf and loop bound. The binding is not only practical, but also unusually utilitarian in feel—both Design Typography and its client were keen to ensure that the publication reflected the detailing of the development and wasn't dismissed as a predictably glossy promotion. The grid is based on eight small columns that can be used in different combinations to accommodate text, images, maps, plans, and diagrams.

Contemporary architecture and spacious layouts dominate the feel of the new build apartments at L'École. Building in a U-shape around the communal courtyard garden has given the development a real sense of community.

The Winter Gardens add a unique focal feature to the front elevation, providing a fabulous enclosed glass space all year round, offering seclusion and serenity in this bustling London borough.

At the top of the buildings sit the stunning penthouses, whose abundant use of glass ensures they are always flooded with light. The penthouse lifestyle offered at L'École is one of true indulgence – whilst relaxing on the terrace, one can enjoy panoramic views across Islington.

Crafted by CARROT.

KITCHENS
- Individual Swedish-designed black high-gloss 'Kvanum' kitchens combined with white 'Corian' worktops
- Fully integrated 'Siemens' appliances: dishwasher, fridge freezer, ceramic hob, oven & extractor hood

BATHROOMS
- Underfloor electric heating
- 'Porcelanosa' porcelain floor & wall tiles in 'Cube Nature'

BEDROOMS
- Bespoke floor to ceiling wardrobes in master bedrooms
- Satellite TV point
- Telephone socket
- Wall lights
- Carpets

GENERAL
- Oak wide-board floors
- Fully wired for home entertainment system installation

SPECIFICATION

Throughout L'École, detail and finish are second to none and this is synonymous with the Carrot brand and concept. Each L'École apartment is individually crafted by Carrot with precise attention to detail using high-quality materials to the highest level of specification.

Crafted by CARROT.

Q – WHERE IS L'ÉCOLE SITUATED? **A – JUST 2 STOPS AWAY FROM PARIS ON THE EUROSTAR**

ALL THAT YOU WILL EVER NEED …
Whether it is a theatre, university,
museum, green space, antique shop or
good transport links that you need, living
at L'École will ensure that it is right on
your doorstep.

1 King's Cross St Pancras, Eurostar
2 Arsenal, Highbury Fields,
   Metropolitan University
3 Upper Street, N1 Shopping Centre,
   Business Design Centre, Almeida
   Theatre, Antiques Arcade
4 Sadler's Wells Theatre, Exmouth
   Market, Clerkenwell
5 The City, St Paul's
6 Camden Passage Market
7 Hampstead Heath
8 Tate Modern, London Eye
9 Regent's Park
10 2012 Olympic Site

CARROT®   Carrot Limited is a
niche property developer
specialising in bespoke residential and mixed use
schemes in city centres – creating inspiring urban
homes which focus on space and design quality.

Carrot was formed in 2001 by Tim Carr. Tim has been
in the Central London property business since 1975, by
way of estate agencies and consultancy, with a particular
dexterity in acting for developers and house builders in
acquisitions, site disposal and marketing.
Prior to setting up Carrot, Tim co-founded CVZ. For
the past 12 years his management of CVZ has ensured
that it has built a reputation as a 'class act' in urban
regeneration and warehouse conversions, notably in
Clerkenwell, London.
Tim founded Urban Construction Management Ltd
(UCM) in 2001, the construction company for all Carrot
projects. This relationship ensures a tighter control of
the cost and management of the construction process,
allowing Carrot to exercise 'hands-on' control of its
schemes. Since formation, UCM have consistently
delivered projects on budget and to planned timescales.

Central London is Carrot's core market. However
Bristol in the South West, where Carrot is already
developing, has been identified as having similar
regeneration potential and market characteristics,
allowing the Company's expertise to be fruitfully applied
in a new city.

For more information about L'École and other
developments, please contact Charlotte Steedman.

Carrot Ltd
48 Britton Street
London EC1M 5UL
T +44 (0)20 7251 3999
F +44 (0)20 7251 8008
E charlottesteedman@carrotltd.com
www.lecolecarrot.com

Grids: Creative Solutions for Graphic Designers

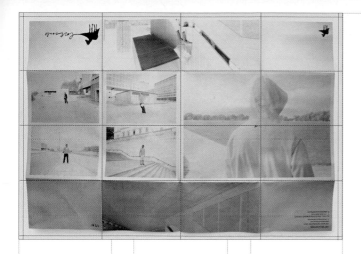

LOST SOULS LOOKBOOK

Design: Julian Harriman-Dickinson at Harriman Steel

The humble postcard was the inspiration behind this promotional "lookbook" for Lost Souls clothing company, designed by Julian Harriman-Dickinson. Consisting of four postcards inserted into the folds of a double-sided A3 (297 × 420mm [11¾ × 16½in]) poster, the overall design utilizes the grid generated by the folding process. Graphic-design grids are generally invisible to the end user and, although determined by format, are additions to it. Here the grid is completely visible and inseparable from the format. This reinterpretation of the grid is, by its nature, three-dimensional, and creates unexpected relationships between text and image as the structure unfolds and the content is revealed.

GRID SPECIFICATIONS

Page size (trimmed)	167 x 193mm
Top margin	7mm
Bottom margin	7mm
Outside margin	9mm
Inside margin	12mm
Number of columns	5
Gutter width	4mm
Extras	6 horizontal fields

TIME WARNER CABLE SAN DIEGO MAILER

Design: Saima Malik at Origin Design

Origin was briefed to design direct mail that would capture the dynamism of southern California and help revitalize Time Warner's business-to-business brand image in the region. To accentuate the forward-looking ambition of his client, designer Jim Mousner used a slanting grid, and introduced angled columns along with images cropped to fit oblique abstract forms. Cleverly, the rotated grid is mirrored horizontally across the top and bottom of the page so that arrow-like shapes are created where columns and shapes meet. The dynamic is further emphasized through the use of angled die-cuts, bold typography, and double-hit fluorescent colors.

GRID SPECIFICATIONS

Page size (trimmed)	784.225 x 171.45mm
Top margin	7.938mm
Bottom margin	7.938mm
Outside margin	7.938mm
Inside margin	7.938mm
Number of columns	4, interior at 141.5° rotation
Gutter width	1.588mm
Extras	2 horizontal fields

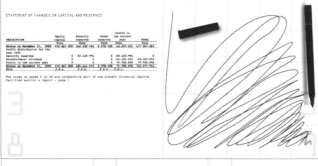

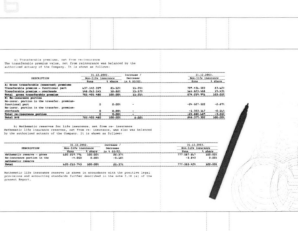

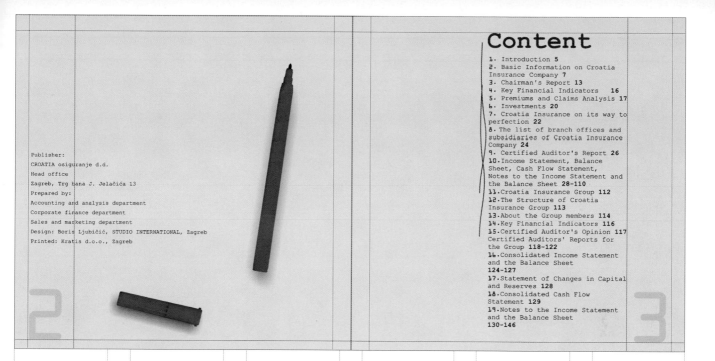

Publisher:
CROATIA osiguranje d.d.
Head office
Zagreb, Trg bana J. Jelačića 13
Prepared by:
Accounting and analysis department
Corporate finance department
Sales and marketing department
Design: Boris Ljubičić, STUDIO INTERNATIONAL, Zagreb
Printed: Kratis d.o.o., Zagreb

Content

1. Introduction **5**
2. Basic Information on Croatia Insurance Company **7**
3. Chairman's Report **13**
4. Key Financial Indicators **16**
5. Premiums and Claims Analysis **17**
6. Investments **20**
7. Croatia Insurance on its way to perfection **22**
8. The list of branch offices and subsidiaries of Croatia Insurance Company **24**
9. Certified Auditor's Report **26**
10. Income Statement, Balance Sheet, Cash Flow Statement, Notes to the Income Statement and the Balance Sheet **28-110**
11. Croatia Insurance Group **112**
12. The Structure of Croatia Insurance Group **113**
13. About the Group members **114**
14. Key Financial Indicators **116**
15. Certified Auditor's Opinion **117** Certified Auditors' Reports for the Group **118-122**
16. Consolidated Income Statement and the Balance Sheet **124-127**
17. Statement of Changes in Capital and Reserves **128**
18. Consolidated Cash Flow Statement **129**
19. Notes to the Income Statement and the Balance Sheet **130-146**

GRID SPECIFICATIONS

Page size (trimmed)	210 x 210mm
Top margin	10.3mm
Bottom margin	5.3mm
Outside margin	8mm
Inside margin	11.5mm
Number of columns	2
Gutter width	N/A
Extras	N/A

CROATIA ANNUAL REPORT 2003

Design: Boris Ljubicic at Studio International

Croatia Osiguranje is one of Croatia's most reputable insurance companies. Although it is keen to build on its reputation and long history, the company is aware that its successes have to be presented accessibly. Its annual report is full of complex tabular matter along with facts and figures. Designer Boris Ljubicic's aim was to ensure easy navigation and facilitate understanding of this dense document through simple graphic means. The grid introduces plenty of white space and enables a clear and clean layout of information, text, tables, and charts. The colored-pencil device is a playful and humanizing element used to make hierarchy clear through underlining and highlighting details of the content.

U.S. GREEN BUILDING COUNCIL

ANNUAL REPORT

Grids: Creative Solutions for Graphic Designers

Page size (trimmed)	200.025 x 254mm
Top margin	2.54mm
Bottom margin	22.225mm
Outside margin	6.35mm
Inside margin	6.35mm
Number of columns	3
Gutter width	N/A
Extras	N/A

U.S. GREEN BUILDING COUNCIL
ANNUAL REPORT
Design: Richard Chartier

Richard Chartier wanted the U.S. Green Building Council (USGBC) annual report to be architectural in feel, so decided to use the grid as a metaphor for construction. His solution was to "build" the design so that it gradually reveals its own supporting architecture—a grid of vertical columns and horizontal fields. This idea is developed throughout the publication and its various supplements, including a financial insert in which the baseline grid is exposed. Chartier also introduced a variety of illustrative elements, juxtaposing them with his clean, abstract grid to emphasize the relationship between man-made and natural structures.

Exhibitions

ON-SITE
ARQUITECTURA CONTEMPORÁNEA
EN LA COMUNIDAD DE MADRID

GRID SPECIFICATIONS

Page size (trimmed)	Resizable, as required
Top margin	½ base unit
Bottom margin	½ base unit
Outside margin	½ base unit
Inside margin	½ base unit
Number of columns	Flexible
Gutter width	2.5mm
Extras	Grid developed from base unit—hexagon

ON-SITE EXHIBITION GUIDELINES
Design: BaseDESIGN

The exhibition On-Site: New Architecture in Spain documented recent Spanish architectural innovation. A Museum of Modern Art initiative, the exhibition opened in New York before moving to Madrid. BaseDESIGN's graphic solution uses the architectonic form of a cube (suggested by the perspective of the hexagon) as a basis for the identity. The three visible sides of the cube symbolize the exhibition, tours, and talks, which are also color-coded as red, blue, and green, respectively. Although not a conventional typographic grid, this is a highly flexible modular system that provides the framework for a range of color and pattern combinations to communicate the diversity in form, scale, and geography of the exhibits.

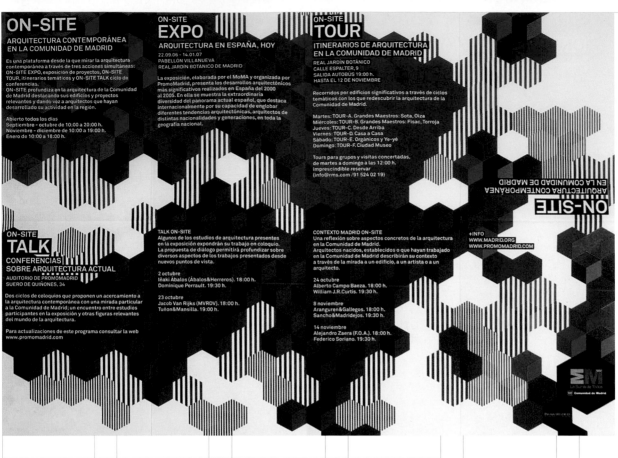

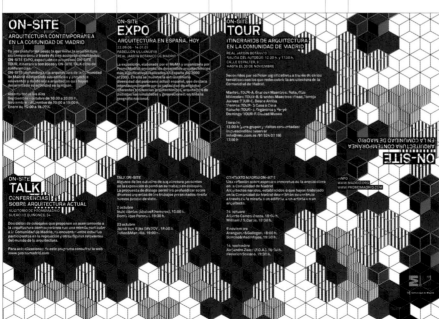

ON-SITE
TOUR
TOUR-A
GRANDES MAESTROS:
SOTA, OIZA

ON-SITE
TOUR
TOUR-A
GRANDES MAESTROS:
SOTA, OIZA

TORRES BLANCAS

Francisco Javier Sáenz de Oíza
1961-1968
Avenida de América, 37

Juan Huarte, promotor y gran mecenas de la arquitectura madrileña de los sesenta, quiso construir un nuevo modelo de residencias en altura. Siguiendo las ideas de Le Corbusier, Oíza propuso un proyecto ideal de torre que tuviera todas las ventajas de las viviendas unifamiliares. Decidió apilar un conjunto de villas en vertical formando una estructura arbórea, donde las raíces son el acceso semienterrado conectado con la ciudad y prolongado bajo tierra en aparcamientos e instalaciones; las viviendas forman el tronco y la parte alta, las ramas, agrupan todos los elementos sociales de la torre: restaurante, tiendas, piscina, gimnasio, etc., inclusión que permite segregar los usos domésticos en favor de la privacidad, así como optimizar recursos, mejorar la calidad de vida y fomentar el intercambio social.
Originalmente concebida como una pareja de torres, de las que solamente se llevó a cabo una, fue construida con pantallas semicirculares de hormigón armado.
Alrededor del núcleo central de comunicaciones se disponen cuatro viviendas por planta, algunas en dúplex, todas con amplios balcones semicirculares que amplifican el límite entre el interior y el exterior, dotando al conjunto de una gran expresividad plástica desarrollada en la Basílica de Aránzazu y culminada en Torres Blancas, convertidas voluntariamente en uno de los iconos de la arquitectura madrileña.

No te pierdas...
todo el edificio, cada una de sus esquinas merece la pena: la piscina, el restaurante, los apartamentos, el portal, los núcleos de comunicación...

→ Metro Línea 7 Cartagena

TORRES BLANCAS

Francisco Javier Sáenz de Oíza
1961-1968
Avenida de América, 37

Juan Huarte, promotor y gran mecenas de la arquitectura madrileña de los sesenta, quiso construir un nuevo modelo de residencias en altura. Siguiendo las ideas de Le Corbusier, Oíza propuso un proyecto ideal de torre que tuviera todas las ventajas de las viviendas unifamiliares. Decidió apilar un conjunto de villas en vertical formando una estructura arbórea, donde las raíces son el acceso semienterrado conectado con la ciudad y prolongado bajo tierra en aparcamientos e instalaciones; las viviendas forman el tronco y la parte alta, las ramas, agrupan todos los elementos sociales de la torre: restaurante, tiendas, piscina, gimnasio, etc., inclusión que permite segregar los usos domésticos en favor de la privacidad, así como optimizar recursos, mejorar la calidad de vida y fomentar el intercambio social.
Originalmente concebida como una pareja de torres, de las que solamente se llevó a cabo una, fue construida con pantallas semicirculares de hormigón armado.
Alrededor del núcleo central de comunicaciones se disponen cuatro viviendas por planta, algunas en dúplex, todas con amplios balcones semicirculares que amplifican el límite entre el interior y el exterior, dotando al conjunto de una gran expresividad plástica desarrollada en la Basílica de Aránzazu y culminada en Torres Blancas, convertidas voluntariamente en uno de los iconos de la arquitectura madrileña.

No te pierdas...
todo el edificio, cada una de sus esquinas merece la pena: la piscina, el restaurante, los apartamentos, el portal, los núcleos de comunicación...

→ Metro Línea 7 Cartagena

ON-SITE
ARQUITECTURA CONTEMPORÁNEA
EN LA COMUNIDAD DE MADRID

ON-SITE
EXPO
ARQUITECTURA EN ESPAÑA, HOY
22.09.06 - 14.01.07
PABELLÓN VILLANUEVA
REAL JARDÍN BOTÁNICO DE MADRID

ON-SITE
TOUR
ITINERARIOS DE ARQUITECTURA
EN LA COMUNIDAD DE MADRID

ON-SITE
TALK
CONFERENCIAS
SOBRE ARQUITECTURA ACTUAL

+INFO: WWW.PROMOMADRID.COM

26 June — 06 July 2003   SEA-Gallery
An exhibition of original posters designed by Wim Crouwel for the Stedelijk
Museum, Amsterdam.

WIM CROUWEL EXHIBITION CATALOG
Design: SEA

SEA self-published this catalog to accompany an exhibition of Wim Crouwel posters held at its gallery in London. Renowned for his fascination with grid structures and a systematic approach to design, Crouwel's posters juxtapose highly structured letterforms, often hand-drawn, with carefully composed typographic layouts. SEA's catalog uses a nine-column grid divided horizontally into 11 fields. This structure gives great flexibility while ensuring unity throughout the publication. Columns are joined in different combinations to allow for varying text measures. Both images and text hang at different heights determined by the fields. By leaving columns and fields empty, SEA has used space creatively to add emphasis and to help the reader navigate the page.

Fernand Léger

Silkscreen, 88x60cm
Stedelijk Van
Abbemuseum
Eindhoven
1957

stedelijk
van abbemuseum
eindhoven

fernand leger

dagelijks geopend
van 10-17 uur
zondag
van 13-17 uur
dinsdag- en
donderdagavond
van 20-22 uur

2 februari tot
10 maart 1957

Mason Wells
North Design

06 — 07

I was disappointed that I had to comment on the Léger poster, not because I dislike it, but because I wanted to pay homage to Vormgevers (a personal favourite, and I hazard a guess, the one everyone else wanted to pass comment on). But examining an early piece such as this allows one to re-assess things in terms of the evolution of Crouwel's work.

It goes without saying that Crouwel's posters meet all the right criteria in terms of what constitutes a good poster — they are legible, they work at varying proximities, they are compositionally perfect and they are built on content. You almost take it for granted that all the right bits are in the right places.

What really makes his work so outstanding, is the custom letterforms and typefaces (which feature in seven of the eight posters on display). In the case of the Léger poster, the title is created as an interlocking linear structure, presumably in reference to the cubist forms of the artist. This would be easy on a Mac, but three decades before, it brought along a new set of problems.

Crouwel placed no boundaries on himself and his constant re-invention of typeforms (whether manipulated or drawn from scratch) kept his work free from the dogmas associated with the work of many of his contemporaries, ensuring that each new artwork was fresh. Looking at this poster, it's easy to see how it pre-empts his later work such as Vormgevers, Visuele communicatie and New Alphabet.

What is hard to comment on are the bits that contextualise it. Tangible elements such as colour, print process and scale — even mistakes such as misaligned registration and over-specified colour trap — become impossible to pass comment on when all one has as reference are miniscule reproductions (in this case an absolutely knackered Mode en Module and a few Dutch design books). It's like criticising a piece of architecture without visiting the building — you have to go there and experience it to truly understand it.

Fernand Léger

Silkscreen, 88x60cm
Stedelijk Van
Abbemuseum
Eindhoven
1957

Mason Wells
North Design

I was disappointed that I had to comment on the Léger poster, not because I dislike it, but because I wanted to pay homage to Vormgevers (a personal favourite, and I hazard a guess, the one everyone else wanted to pass comment on). But examining an early piece such as this allows one to re-assess things in terms of the evolution of Crouwel's work.

It goes without saying that Crouwel's posters meet all the right criteria in terms of what constitutes a good poster — they are legible, they work at varying proximities, they are compositionally perfect and they are built on content. You almost take it for granted that all the right bits are in the right places.

What really makes his work so outstanding, is the custom letterforms and typefaces (which feature in seven of the eight posters on display). In the case of the Léger poster, the title is created as an interlocking linear structure, presumably in reference to the cubist forms of the artist. This would be easy on a Mac, but three decades before, it brought along a new set of problems.

Crouwel placed no boundaries on himself and his constant re-invention of typeforms (whether manipulated or drawn from scratch) kept his work free from the dogmas associated with the work of many of his contemporaries, ensuring that each new artwork was fresh. Looking at this poster, it's easy to see how it pre-empts his later work such as Vormgevers, Visuele communicatie and New Alphabet.

What is hard to comment on are the bits that contextualise it. Tangible elements such as colour, print process and scale — even mistakes such as misaligned registration and over-specified colour trap — become impossible to pass comment on when all one has as reference are miniscule reproductions (in this case an absolutely knackered Mode en Module and a few Dutch design books). It's like criticising a piece of architecture without visiting the building — you have to go there and experience it to truly understand it.

GRID SPECIFICATIONS

Page size (trimmed)	210 x 265mm
Top margin	5mm
Bottom margin	5mm
Outside margin	10mm
Inside margin	10mm
Number of columns	9
Gutter width	2.5mm
Extras	11 horizontal fields

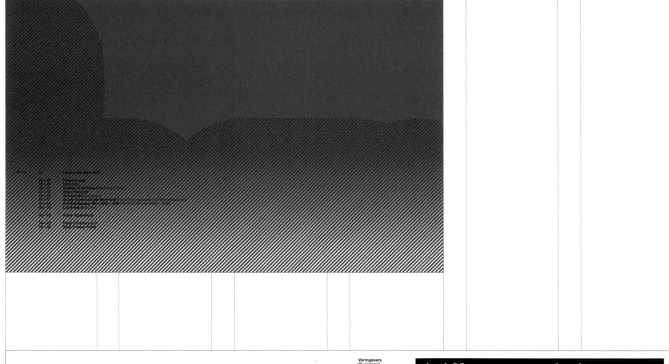

Vormgevers
(Designers)

Offset, 95x64cm
Stedelijk Museum,
Amsterdam
1968

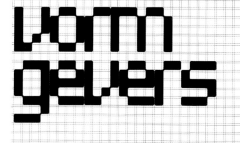

Mark Holt
Mark Holt Design

14 — 15

For this poster, Crouwel revealed the grid he had used on all his previous posters (and the later posters he would produce) for the Stedelijk Museum. Place a number of Stedelijk posters alongside Vormgevers and it is remarkable to see the grid used time and time again to anchor each poster's design elements.

Each grid square and corresponding interval is equal to five units, which predetermines the height of the two sizes of font used on Vormgevers. The diameter of the rounded corners of the larger font, is equal to the width of a single unit. The font's form grows out of the grid itself, letter and grid are one. Resolved it certainly is. And if anyone needed proof that black and white need not be a poverty then surely this poster is it.

My favourite detail? The numeral five which starts the second text line, set to the x-height of the font and placed directly under the 's' of Stedelijk. In this context, quite possibly the most bizarre five I think I've ever seen.

22 — 23

Fernand Léger
1957

Hiroshima
1957

Beelden in Het Heden
1959

Edgar Fernhout
1963

Vormgevers
1968

Visuele Communicatie
Nederland
1968

Het Nederlandse Affice
1890 — 1968
1968

Lucht/Kunst
1971

One of Crouwel's best known posters, and a personal favourite of his. Drawn without the aid of graph paper, the poster's strong diagonal black lines reveal Crouwel's initial point of reference — it was a continuation from his New Acquisitions poster of 1956.

The Léger poster is simply constructed, with a letter 'r' which is formed from part of a pure circle, rather than being optically corrected.

Crouwel was very impressed by Léger's paintings and he has described this piece as being a typographic, if somewhat poetic, interpretation of the artist's work.

Designed in the same year as the Léger poster, this poster marked an exhibition of Japanese drawings based on Hiroshima. The background colour was similar to that of Japanese lacquer and the word Hiroshima is based on a small Grotesk — the way the letters were constructed determined their very tight spacing.

Crouwel wanted the word Hiroshima to appear heavy and threatening, and likens the ascenders to singed chimneys rising up from the black form.

A poster which was designed for an exhibition of sculpture. Crouwel designed the poster in portrait format to look like a landscape with three vertical sculptures, but it was always hung horizontally by mistake.

The bands of colour represent earth, sky and the horizon and the letterforms form the three sculptures. The letters are tightly spaced and the serifs extended to give the effect of a solid sculpture — they were individually drawn, pushed together and then painstakingly drawn again.

In this poster for an exhibition of paintings by Edgar Fernhout, this poster featured a visible grid that was used for the layouts of all of the catalogues Crouwel designed for the Stedelijk.

The original graph sheets were printed in light grey — for this poster, Crouwel made the lines more visible and composed the letterforms inside them. The letterforms were a precursor to Crouwel's Fodor typeface, which was designed three years later.

One of Crouwel's most talked about pieces, this poster featured a visible grid that was used for the layouts of all of the catalogues Crouwel designed for the Stedelijk.

The original graph sheets were printed in light grey — for this poster, Crouwel made the lines more visible and composed the letterforms inside them. The letterforms were a precursor to Crouwel's Fodor typeface, which was designed three years later.

Designed for the Dutch Art Directors Club, this poster combines simplified pointed letterforms, all three points wide, which sit on a background inspired by the first bar codes.

The letterforms were reduced to very simple forms and are similar to those in Crouwel's soft alphabet, designed for his Claes Oldenburg poster of 1970.

Although it is a poster about visual communication, Crouwel admits that it is the most illegible poster that he has made.

This poster was created for an exhibition about posters and features a folded down corner in the top left hand side, which reveals the Stedelijk marque and is a reference to the transient nature of the artform.

The letterforms are constructed around a square, and give rise to a strong sense of perspective, creating striking diagonals. The letters that form the word 'Affiche' go off the page on both sides, suggesting a fleeting glimpse of a poster as you walk past it.

This poster is for an exhibition that was devoted to art made with air — pieces that were inflatable. Crouwel rounded off the letterforms (which are constructed from a narrow Grotesk) and pushed them together to give them a feeling of being blown full of air.

Both the outline and the spaces between the letters become very significant and the speech bubble is another (somewhat more literal) take on the subject matter.

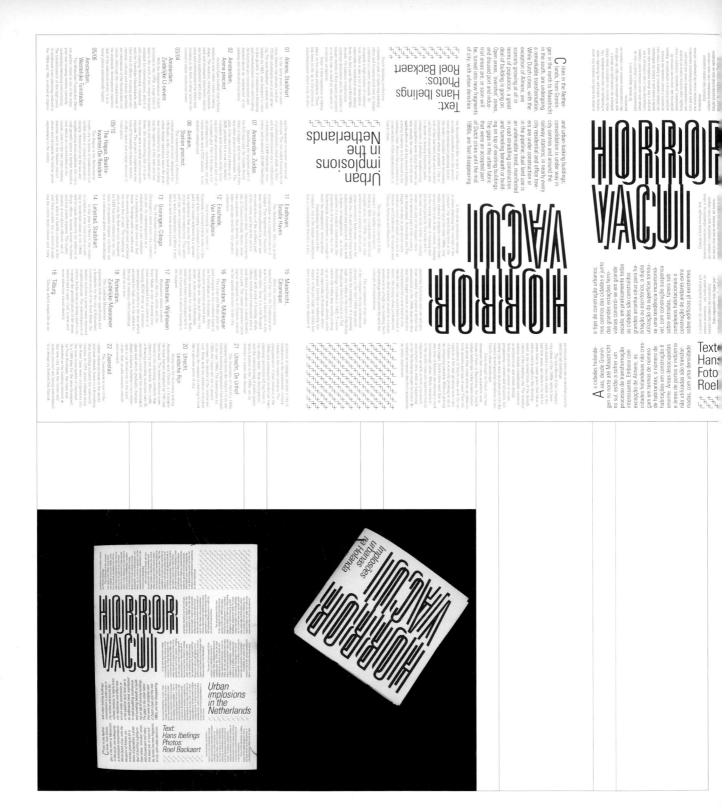

Implosões
urbanas
na Holanda

Texto:
Hans Ibelings
Fotografia:
Roel Backaert

GRID SPECIFICATIONS

Page size (trimmed)	Panels: 1100 x 1100mm/
	Booklet: 170 x 235mm
Top margin	Panels: 52.5mm/Booklet: 7.8mm
Bottom margin	Panels: 200mm/Booklet: 7.8mm
Outside margin	Panels: 52.5mm/Booklet: 7.8mm
Inside margin	Panels: 52.5mm/Booklet: 0mm (interior)
Number of columns	Panels: 5/Booklet: 5 (sideways)
Gutter width	Panels: 30mm/Booklet: 5mm
Extras	N/A

HORROR VACUI EXHIBITION PANELS

Design: Arjan Groot and Julia Müller

These panels and booklet were designed for the traveling
exhibition Horror Vacui: Urban Implosions in the Netherlands,
initially shown at the Lisbon Architecture Triennial. The exhibition
looked at how gaps are filled within the urban fabric of Dutch
cities—the term "horror vacui" translates as "fear of empty spaces."
The designers took this theme as the starting point for their design.
They filled any empty spaces on their pages with a graphic pattern
influenced by textile weavings and Scottish tartans. Reminiscent
of op art, this pattern creates a kind of visual vertigo appropriate
to the overall subject matter. These repetitive graphic marks are,
in themselves, an elaborate grid, and form the basis of the more
conventional typographic grid used for the text and image layouts.

HORROR VACUI

Urban implosions in the Netherlands

Cities in the Netherlands, from Groningen in the north to Maastricht in the south, are undergoing a remarkable transformation. While Dutch cities, with the exception of Almere, are scarcely growing at all in terms of population, a great deal of building is going on. Open areas, 'overshot' zones, and disused port and industrial areas are, or soon will be, turned into new fragments of city, with urban densities and urban-looking buildings; consolidation is under way in city centres and around the railway stations; in nearly every city residential and office towers are under construction or in the pipeline; dual land use is an undeniable trend, manifested in road-straddling construction and tunneling beneath or building on top of existing buildings. The gaps in the urban fabric that were an accepted part of Dutch cities until the mid 1980s, are fast disappearing.

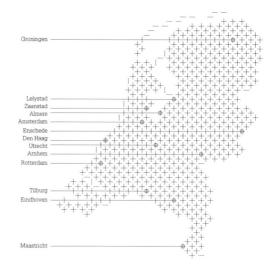

This exhibition is produced by the Netherlands Architecture Institute in collaboration with A10 new European architecture, with financial support from the Netherlands Architecture Fund.

Curators: Hans Ibelings + Kirsten Hannema. Exhibition design: Marta Malé-Alemany + José Pedro Sousa (ReD). Graphic design: Arjan Groot + Julia Müller. Photography: Roel Backaert. Production: Suzanne Kole + Marinke van der Horst. Supervisor: Martien de Vletter. International coordinator: Agnes Wijers

Special thanks to: AAS Architecten, ARCADIS Bouw en Vastgoed BV, Architectenbureau Art Zaaijer, Architectenbureau Marlies Rohmer, Architectuurstudio Herman Hertzberger, Atelier Rijksbouwmeester, Benthem Crouwel Architekten BV, Bouwfonds MAB Development, Bureau B+B stedebouw en landschapsarchitectuur, City of Eindhoven, City of Tilburg, Claus en Kaan Architecten, De Architekten Cie, De Zwarte Hond, Department of Physical Planing and Economic Affairs Groningen, Department of Physical Planning Amsterdam, Dick van Gameren architecten B.V., Dienst Stedelijke Ontwikkeling – City of The Hague, dS+V Rotterdam, (EEA) Erick van Egeraat associated architects, FARO Architecten bv, FPW Rotterdam, hvdn Architecten, JHK Architecten, Jo Coenen & Co Architecten, KCAP Architects&Planners, Köther | Salman | Koedijk | Architecten bv, Meyer en Van Schooten Architecten BV,

MVRDV, NL Architects, OD 205 architectuur bv, Office for Metropolitan Architecture, OMS Beheer bv (City of Lelystad and William Properties bv), ONL [Oosterhuis_Lénárd], Ontwikkelingsbedrijf Rotterdam, Pierre Gautier architecture, PPKS Architects Ltd., Project Organisation Stationsgebied – City of Utrecht, Projectbureau Amsterdam Zuidas – City of Amsterdam, Projectbureau Zuidelijke IJ-oevers – City of Amsterdam, Rijnboutt Van der Vossen Rijnboutt bv, S333 architects, Soeters Van Eldonk Architecten, Stadsdeel Geuzenveld-Slotermeer – City of Amsterdam, Tania Concko Architectes, THALEN/BASELINE, UN Studio, Van Sambeek & Van Veen Architecten, Vera Yanovshtchinsky architecten, vof ontwikkelingscombinatie IMA (ING, MOESbouw, AM), West 8 urban design & landscape architecture b.v., Wiel Arets Architects, Ymere Ontwikkeling, Zwarts & Jansma Architects

Groningen   Ciboga

Rotterdam   Wijnhaven

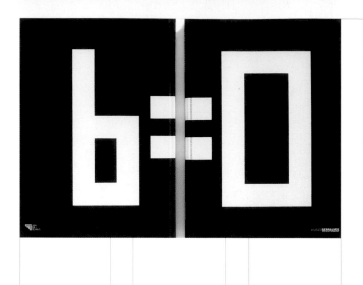

considerada então como «demasiado *engagé*». Tendo por objectivo único transformar-se num agrupamento «completamente atrasado mental», logo ficou decidido que os Ena Pá deveriam assumir como seu objectivo fazer a «pior música possível», utilizando apenas um ou dois acordes, a qual seria ainda servida por letras «absolutamente idiotas». Procurariam a todo o custo transformar-se num grupo de rock português que, «tal como os Sex Pistols ou os Ramones», exibisse a sua «mediocridade de modo transbordante e esplendoroso». A ideia fez o seu caminho, que deve já aqui ficar enunciado. Na futura formação musical, espécie de braço musical da homeostética, esteve, além de Vieira, Francisco Ferro. O primeiro concerto, ou melhor, a primeira «representação de concerto rock», aconteceria ainda em Dezembro de 1982 – no meio de uma festa operária e num prédio em construção, a ela tendo apenas assistido Portugal, Proença, uma rapariga anónima e seu cão – e o disco inicial viria a ser publicado cinco anos depois: trata-se de um single em vinil com duas músicas apenas,

«Pão, Amor e Totobola» e «Telephone call». A partir de 1984, muitas das canções dos Ena Pá 2000 passaram a ser escritas por Fernando Brito, ao lado de Manuel Vieira. Em Anelhe, os passeios pelo campo e as imensas refeições, naquele Verão de 1982, foram intercaladas também com a realização de várias pinturas. Pedro Portugal, que desde aí se atribuiu no movimento o papel do sujeito que cola as partes e as faz operar – «os budistas chamam a estas pessoas pontes», assinala a propósito –, começou a registar fotograficamente todas estas viagens, bem como as performances efectuadas pelos seis artistas e companheiros na ESBAL, daí resultando um acervo composto por milhares de negativos de «fotos oficiais» ou «autorizadas». E é facto indesmentível que a memória homeostética adquire, através das fotografias de Pedro Portugal, uma extensão

desconhecida de outros agrupamentos estéticos. Os três passaram ainda pelo festival de Vilar de Mouros, onde viriam a conhecer as irmãs Medeiros, Maria e Inês, que pouco depois começariam a aparecer no Grupo de Teatro da Escola de Belas-Artes, animado por Xana e que viria também a ser integrado por Vieira e Proença. Estes dois partiriam, ainda em meados de Agosto, para o Algarve e em Lagos – onde se encontrava Xana de férias – tocaram bandolim e guitarra nas ruas durante dias seguidos, tendo com isso conseguido arrecadar algumas moedas. Rumaram em seguida à Fuzeta, localidade em que lhes surgiria a personagem Capitão Nemo, cujas cartas, relatando viagens imaginárias, foram escritas num espírito de absoluta descoberta. No mês seguinte, Vieira e Portugal foram até Paris tirar mais fotografias e ver o que «estava a acontecer».

GRID SPECIFICATIONS

Page size (trimmed)	252 x 356mm
Top margin	15mm
Bottom margin	15mm
Outside margin	25mm
Inside margin	15mm
Number of columns	12
Gutter width	4mm
Extras	Baseline grid, 14pt

6 = O EXHIBITION CATALOG

Design: Lizá Ramalho, Artur Rebelo, and Nuno Bastos at R2 design

This catalog accompanied an exhibition by 1980s Portuguese
art collective Homeosteticos, held at the Serralves Museum
of Contemporary Art, Porto. The title, 6=0, reflected how under-
appreciated this group of six artists felt. Designers Lizá Ramalho,
Artur Rebelo, and Nuno Bastos emphasized this notion by reversing
the equation of the title and placing a zero on the front cover and
a six on the back.

Illustrated books

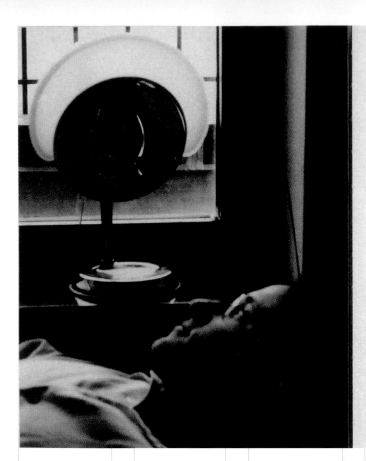

The Art of the Jester

Chip Kidd. Photograph by Duane Michals, 2001.

Pull a book at random from your bookcase and look at its cover. That is all you need to do to travel back to that specific moment in your life when you first read it. As compact as a time capsule, a book jacket holds forever the memory of the brief cultural period when it was in print. But a short shelf life is the price a book jacket must pay for leaving a vivid impression in the mind. My 1987 hardcover edition of Tom Wolfe's *The Bonfire of The Vanities*, so promising when it came out during the heady days of the Reagan administration, looks and feels today like a dear old friend wearing a toupee.[1] However, the fact that most book jackets look dated within a couple of years of their publication does not take anything away from their graphic appeal. One of the things we love about books is the way they age along with us.

Yet today, newness is considered a critical design element of a book jacket. Indeed, when I survey bookstores, the future obsolescence of the latest best-sellers' covers is the furthest thing from my mind. Even though I am aware that the current jackets will one day have the same emotional patina as award-winning jackets designed or art directed a decade ago by Louise Fili, Carin Goldberg, Sara Eisenman, Paula Scher, Frank Metz, Krystyna Skalski, Fred Marcellino or Neil Stuart, I cannot help but be seduced by the allure of instant modernity that the new books seem to capture. One of the things that tells me that a book is brand new is the presence of photography on its cover. Over the last couple of years, I have been conditioned to equate the use of conceptual photography on American book jackets with cutting-edge, contemporary literature. In contrast, if a book has an illustrated jacket, I regret to admit that I assume that its content is somewhat behind the curve. Graphic profiling, like racial profiling, is an inescapable reality in the world in which we live today.

The now popular photographic approach was originally pioneered in the late 1980s by a group of young designers working for the Knopf Publishing Group. Famous for its emblematic Borzoi logo, the Knopf

MONOGRAPHICS

Donnie Brasco

Director – Mike Newell, 1997
Titles – Kyle Cooper (dir.)
for Imaginary Forces

One of the first main titles to be done under the imaginary forces name, Donnie Brasco is a sub-narrative as moody and intensive that it had one less issue only passing it along the film itself. Using a combination of predominantly black and white and colour stills shot in surveillance style complete with Kodak markings and grease-pencil scribblings – Cooper choreographs an unsettling sequence about friendship, betrayal and the implosion of relationships caught in the middle. Accompanied by a delicate piece of music to facilitate, the gritty still images become animated thanks to a carefully choreographed edit that forces slow motion punctuated by rapid cut action sequences and the occasional piece of footage. The title begins and ends with a view of Johnny Depp's dark-ringed eyes looking from outside – an imposing cop in the midst of New York wise guys.

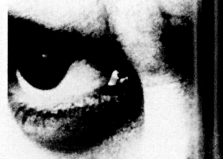
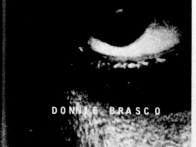

DONNIE BRASCO

GRID SPECIFICATIONS

Page size (trimmed)	189 x 238mm
Top margin	5mm
Bottom margin	10mm
Outside margin	8mm
Inside margin	18mm
Number of columns	6
Gutter width	5mm
Extras	Baseline grid, 13.25pt starting at 45.5mm

MONOGRAPHICS SERIES

Design: Brad Yendle at Design Typography

Each book in Laurence King's Monographics series concentrates on the work of one creative practitioner. The series style has to be recognizable, but flexible, and has to act as a fairly neutral backdrop to the work featured. These considerations informed designer Brad Yendle's decision to create what he describes as a considered, but quite austere design. Herbert Spencer's *Typographica* magazine and the *Graphis* annuals from the 1960s were his inspiration. Yendle's grid is a multicolumn structure that can accommodate continuous text, captions, and index easily. Its large top margin introduces welcome breathing space to pages that include visual examples and formats from a range of disciplines—movie stills and titles, book covers and spreads, prints and comic books.

Véronique Vienne

Chip Kidd

Laurence King Publishing

Through the Glass Darkly

Kyle Cooper. Photograph by Michael Power.

Kyle Cooper is a postmodern paradox. He is an iconoclast who loves what he transgresses, whether the tenets of modernist typography, the idea of apple-pie America or even the belief in an all-loving, all-powerful God. He is by nature betwixt and between, not quite fitting into the commercial world of Hollywood and not entirely at home in the realm of high-design discourse. He is a true-believing Christian whose oeuvre has often lingered on the sinister themes of murder and madness. The work that he has created over the past decade – first at R/Greenberg and then at Imaginary Forces, the studio he cofounded in 1996 with Peter Frankfurt and Chip Houghton – distinctively plays off this tension to great effect.

In an age predicated on irony – the knowing collusion between auteur and audience via winking references made at breakneck speed – Cooper's work comes into bold relief, for it is marked by something that seems all but lost in our cleverness-as-king culture: earnestness. This may sound an odd description for a designer who first came to fame with the opening titles for David Fincher's 1995 film Seven, a sequence characterized by degraded, hand-scrawled type and nerve-jangling imagery. But Cooper has realized something important: desecration is all the more effective when the ideals being torn down are ones that are dearly held by the desecrater.

Kyle Cooper's short-form artistry is particularly appreciated in a culture known for its collective attention deficit disorder because it delivers intense experiences in quick bursts. The fact that such jags of entertainment have snuck into the unassuming cultural spaces of legally mandated credit sequences is a testament to both the creative urge and, perhaps, consumer culture's discomfort in the presence of blank, unmediated space. Cooper himself displays a tendency toward fitful absorption – darting associatively in conversation from one topic to the next, multi-tasking to such an extent that many of the interviews that fill his dictionary-sized book of press clippings were given on his cell phone while driving the freeways of Los Angeles

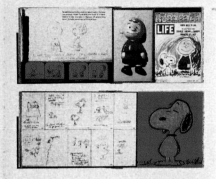

The luxury quality of Kidd's art
direction in these spreads from Peanuts
is reminiscent of a family photo album.
Changes of scale give the pages their
texture. The comic strips are photographed
from the original pulp pages, showing
wear and tear and discolouration, because
Schulz didn't have anything that could be
called an archive in his studio, scavenging
this book was like a scavenger hunt for
Kidd and Spear.

104

105

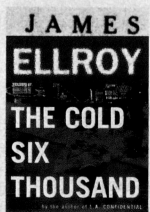

The Cold Six Thousand
James Ellroy
Main photograph – Mell Kilpatrick
2001 New York ALFRED A. KNOPF
[Hardback]

48

The blurred colour photograph of a neon
Las Vegas landscape sets the location for
a tale of violence and corruption amid the
desert casinos. The bloodied crime scene
offers a macabre invitation to enter a world
peopled with amoral characters who both
repel and fascinate.

White Jazz
James Ellroy
Photograph – Robert Morrow
1992 New York ALFRED A. KNOPF
[Hardback]

"Chip Kidd frames the front cover in
pristine white – a colour at once stark,
innocent and inviting. Centered in that
white expanse, an LAPD patrol car door
shot full of holes. The potential book
buyer/reader has been presented with
a statement and a challenge – forceful,
simple, elegant: Read This Book!"
– James Ellroy

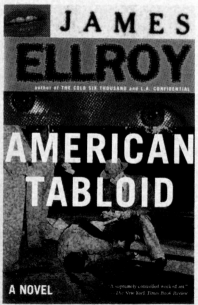

American Tabloid
James Ellroy
Main photograph – Mell Kilpatrick
2001 New York ALFRED A. KNOPF
[Paperback]

49

The saturated and grainy colour images
of eyes and lips highlight our voyeuristic
attraction to scenes of bloodshed and
mayhem. The vintage shot of a crime
scene makes reference to the American
underworld in the years before and after
the Bay of Pigs.

A New Style:
American Design at Mid-Century 1950–1959

'Modern businessmen have come to recognize that design can and should be used to express the character and identity of business organizations. Design is a function of management, both within an industry and the world outside it. Industry is the institution that reaches further into our civilization than government and therefore has a greater opportunity and responsibility to influence the quality of life.'

Herbert Bayer quoted in *A Tribute to Herbert Bayer*, 1979

THE AMERICAN SCENE

The American economy continued to boom in the 1950s. Despite the 'police action' in Korea, Americans generally knew peace, prosperity and conformity in this decade. The nation had a certain naïvety, a simple and optimistic approach to life which preceded the turbulent changes to come in the 1960s. It was the calm before the storm. Improved mass-market technology made television sets affordable for many more people and brought advertising for a vast range of products straight into people's homes. Strikingly different product forms became available. The critic Thomas Hine referred to the 1950s as a time when 'everything from a T-bird to a toaster took on a shape that seemed to lean forward, ready to surge ahead. It was as if the streamlined Art Deco style of the 1930s had been updated for a new audience.' Detroit produced cars with exaggerated tail fins and gleaming chrome.

But despite the bright and shining optimism, the early 1950s were also the era of the McCarthy Communist witch hunts, the beginning of a deep dissent in the land – a conflict between liberalism and xenophobic conservatism. Jack Kerouac's book *On The Road* (1957) and Allen Ginsberg's poetry gave voice to the underground counter-culture of the Beat Generation. Music lost its squeaky-clean image and became dissonant and more subversive. Art became more expressive and abstract. The definition of art was even challenged by Claes Oldenberg's soft sculptures and Allan Kaprow's 'Happenings'. The art of New York finally eclipsed that of Paris – the Americans had arrived on the scene with a vengeance. The 1950s was the decade that saw the emergence of the painter Jackson Pollock. His work grew out of a dynamic, improvisational Zeitgeist that characterized both the progressive Jazz of the time and the writings of the Beat Generation. Socially, the beginnings of the civil rights movement happened in 1950 as Rosa Parks sparked the bus boycott in Montgomery, Alabama. Signs of deep change were on the horizon as Americans basked in the postwar optimism while they cruised around the new suburbs in their gas-guzzling cars with huge fins on each rear fender.

Opposite top *Portfolio* magazine was a major professional achievement for Alexey Brodovitch. In this experimental arts publication he was able to combine optimum editorial and design quality. This two-page spread from 1951 presented an article on the painter Jackson Pollock. Scale contrast in the photography plus the understated typography combines to create a layout of great elegance.

Opposite bottom Advertising designer Robert Gage worked for Doyle Dane Bernbach, Inc. He produced this ad for the New York rye bread company Levy's. A whole series of similar ads followed, appearing even as late as 1967. These ads represented the simple, direct, humorous and sometimes controversial approach to print advertising that was common in the 1950s.

JACKSON POLLOCK

ADVERTISING IN THE 1950S

By the late 1940s and early 1950s, an increasing consciousness about graphic design and designers was evident because Modernism became more visible on the creative scene. Design became a more dominant force in the corporations and in the advertising business. An important debate occurred between typographic purists and those who believed in excitement and experimentation. The most effective examples of design in the 1950s were able to mediate these differences, excite their readers and be legible. In advertisements, copy was shorter, headlines more brief, and text functioned to support the illustration. Photography, both colour and black-and-white, was the dominant medium of advertising illustration. Creativity was the big word in this decade, especially in advertising. Towards the end of the 1950s, at a New York Art Directors Club conference, keynote speakers stated that designers were now moving away from being just layout men to assuming creative responsibility for the whole job. Many designers opened their own businesses, companies specializing just in graphic design. In corporations, the title 'graphic design' finally meant something. Those who practised this

You don't have to be Jewish

to love Levy's
real Jewish Rye

Contents

1 Extra, ... The Basis for the New: The Cradle of Modernism 1850–1899 — 7

2 A New World Forming: The Impact of Modernism 1900–1919 — 15

3 American Design in Transition: Traditional to Modernism 1920–1939 — 33

4 Into the Design Scene: Modernism Arrives in America 1930–1939 — 47

5 At War and After: The Creative Forties in America 1940–1949 — 83

6 A New Style: American Design at Mid-Century 1950–1959 — 135

7 Design Since Mid-Century: Diversity and Contradiction 1960–1999 — 157

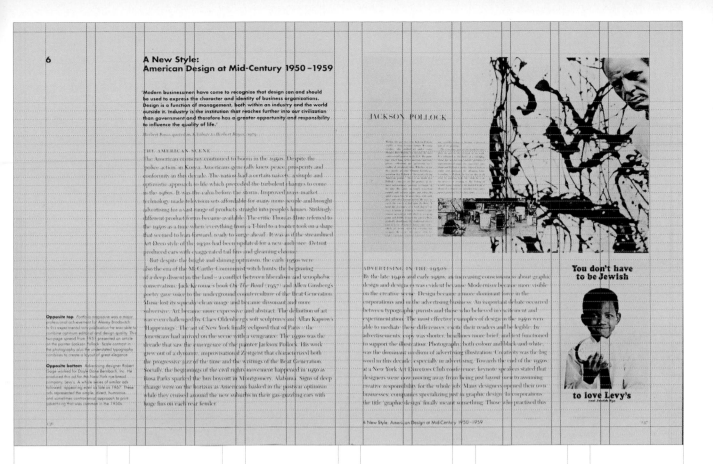

AMERICAN MODERNISM: GRAPHIC DESIGN 1920 TO 1960

Design: Brad Yendle at Design Typography

The design for this book needed to be anonymous and discrete. Many of the designers included now have iconic status—Lester Beall, Alexey Brodovitch, Lou Dorfsman, Paul Rand, Ladislav Sutnar, and Massimo Vignelli—and their work is often extremely bold and strong. The book explores the extraordinary influence that European émigrés had on American design. Appropriately, designer Brad Yendle used two complementary fonts, one designed by a German—Futura —and the other by an American—New Caledonia. Referring to Jost Hochuli's work as a book designer, Yendle developed a six-column grid. By combining these small columns in different configurations, the text, captions, and images are easily accommodated.

GRID SPECIFICATIONS

Page size (trimmed)	280 x 215mm
Top margin	23mm
Bottom margin	27.5mm
Outside margin	15mm
Inside margin	16mm
Number of columns	6
Gutter width	4mm
Extras	Baseline grid, 15.5pt starting at 23mm

AMERICAN
MODERNISM
Graphic Design
1920 to 1960

R. Roger Remington

Of this novel H.G. Wells wrote: *"I do not know how to express the admiration I feel for this wonderful book without seeming to be extravagant. I am not usually lavish with my praise, but indeed the book impresses me as among the very greatest novels I have ever read. It is wholly beautiful; it is saturated with wisdom, and humour and tenderness."*

Growth of the Soil

KNUT HAMSUN

Opposite & below These book jacket designs by Alvin Lustig were produced in the 1940s and early 1950s. Because he designed so many jackets in this period, Lustig experimented widely with style and technique. Some were illustrative, such as *Growth of the Soil* by Knut Hamsun, and others were clearly typographic, such as the *Mind and Heart of Love* by M.C. D'Arcy, *History as the Story of Liberty* by Benedetto Croce and *The Stories* by Willa Cather. Even within his typographic jackets Lustig showed a range of approaches for a good text selection.

Overleaf left Alvin Lustig always wanted to be an architect. He did design several buildings but his career was devoted to many other forms of design as well. He created this cover for *Arts & Architecture* magazine in 1942.

Overleaf right This cover for *Fortune* magazine was designed by Alvin Lustig in 1946. Lustig's use of colour here was attributed to his years in California. This design was interesting because Lustig integrated both flat and dimensional objects on the cover surface.

MONTANA

ONE

Above left The French poster artist Jean Carlu lived in New York during World War II. He designed many advertisements and posters on behalf of the war effort. This ad for the Container Corporation of America was created in 1942. Entitled 'Repaying America's Riches', it represented the CCA's public service support in presenting one million pine tree seedlings to Florida farmers in terms of understandable imagery.

Above right This ad, designed by Paul Rand, ran in consumer magazines in the United States in 1940. It was the first ad in a long series in which each of the 48 United States was featured. The headline read, 'U.S. 48 States light the road to world peace and commerce'. The ad reflected the post World War II optimism for peace and prosperity. Rand's visualization was characteristic in the simplified synthesis of illustration with graphic symbolic form.

talent – tenacity, diplomacy and salesmanship. It is no good to create a beautiful layout if disintegration sets in at any one of the important points of production.[7] In the postwar period, with the economy moving again, more and more Modernist designers were active in producing imaginative advertisements and receiving recognition for bringing fresh, design-oriented solutions to the world of marketing.

GRAPHIC DESIGN ACROSS AMERICA

Two prominent designers, Paul Rand and Bradbury Thompson, emerged during the war and made major contributions to the new direction in American graphic design. They shared an interest in bringing the formal ideas of the European avant-garde into their work at the same time as being firmly grounded in the realities of the American business scene.

Rand, a native New Yorker, worked through the 1940s at the Weintraub Advertising Agency, designing outstanding campaigns for Orbachs, Stafford Fabrics, Disney Hats and others. His covers for *Direction* magazine afforded the opportunity to explore new approaches in form and content interpretation. The covers show Rand's unique understanding of perceptual values, his

Above left Montana was the birth state of E. McKnight Kauffer. He had spent most of his career in England but participated in the Container Corporation of America's 48 States campaign with this ad for his home state in 1944. The CCA ad campaign featured a prominent artist or illustrator from each of the 48 states.

Above right Fernand Léger was a famous French artist who waited out World War II in New York. While he was in the U.S., art directors such as Charles Coiner asked Léger to produce work for Container Corporation of America's ad campaigns. This ad, from 1941, emphasized the fact that the CCA organization was a full-service packaging business. Léger also designed covers for *Fortune* magazine.

Overleaf Between 1947 and 1949, Paul Rand designed a series of ads for Disney Hats. In the campaign, each ad was different but was composed of similar elements, namely a hat, the outline of a figure, the company seal and the copy. This series showed Rand's ingenuity of presenting a visually uninteresting product line with creativity and visual interest.

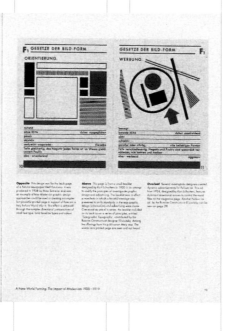

Opposite This design was for the back page of a Futurist newspaper titled *Futurismo*. It was produced in 1926 by Mino Somenzi and was an example of how Modernist graphic design approaches could be used in creating a complex but powerful printed page in support of Fascism in Italy before World War II. The effect is achieved through the complex directional juxtapositions of small text type, bold faced letTypes and colour.

Above This page is from a small booklet designed by Kurt Schwitters in 1930 in an attempt to codify the principles of investigative graphic design and advertising. The booklet was in effect a manifesto in which a bi-cellof meetings was presented to unify standards in the way graphic design information and advertising were made. Conceived as one of a series, the booklet included on its back cover a series of principles, entitled 'Typographic', contributed by the Russian Constructivist designer El Lissitzky. Among his offerings from his publication *Merz* was 'The words on a printed page are seen and not heard.'

Overleaf Several avant-garde designers created dynamic advertisements for *Pelikan* ink. This ad from 1924, designed by Kurt Schwitters, features dominant directional arrows to control the visual flow on the magazine page. Another *Pelikan* ink ad, by the Russian Constructivist El Lissitzky, can be seen on page 29.

A New World Forming: The Impact of Modernism 1900 - 1919   79

GRID SPECIFICATIONS

Page size (trimmed)	260 x 260mm
Top margin	25mm
Bottom margin	27mm
Outside margin	25mm
Inside margin	30mm
Number of columns	4
Gutter width	5mm
Extras	N/A

INDUSTRIAL ROMANTIC

Design: Rian Hughes at Device

Rian Hughes is best known as an illustrator, and a graphic and font designer, but this book focuses on his photographs. It was a challenge to develop a system that would accommodate images with such a variation in size and proportion. Hughes decided to use a square format for the book, which he found sensitive to both portrait and landscape images. His four-column grid had to be used flexibly. Hughes consistently aligned three sides of his photographs with the grid, but allowed one edge to break it, determined by the best crop and scale for that particular shot. He selected the images for each spread based on their relative size as well as their subject matter. The layout is then disrupted by the more randomly placed related ephemera.

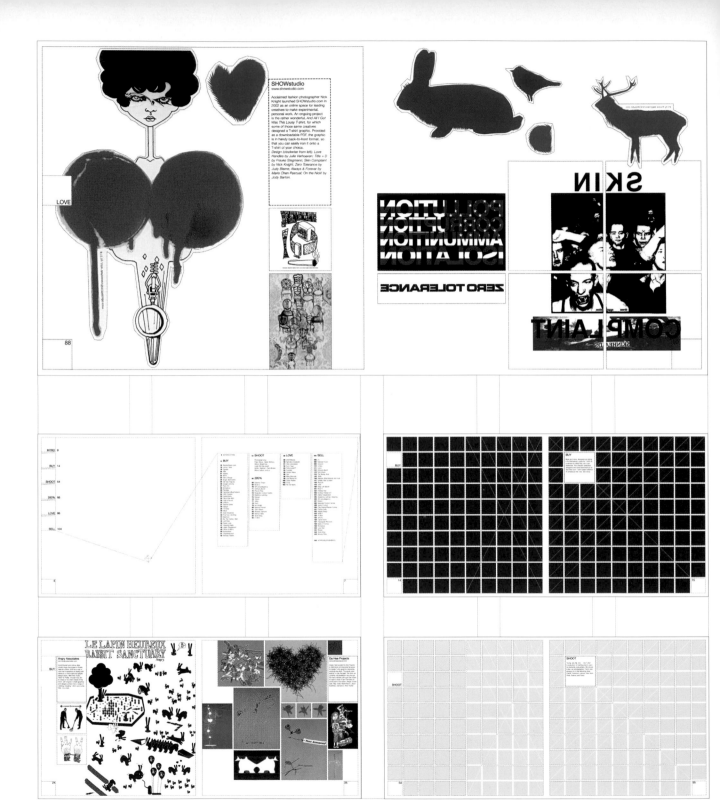

Grids: Creative Solutions for Graphic Designers

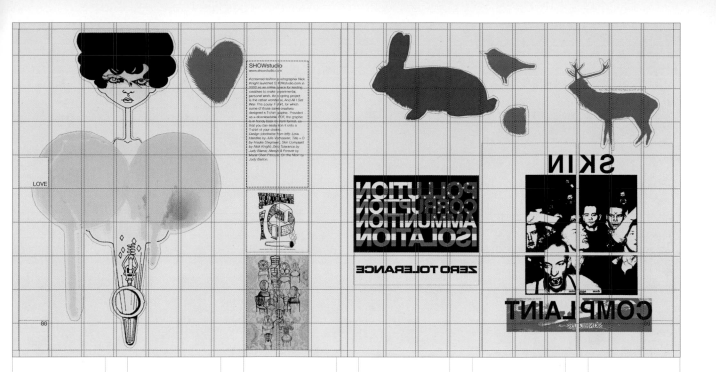

GRID SPECIFICATIONS

Page size (trimmed)	250 x 250mm
Top margin	5mm
Bottom margin	5mm
Outside margin	5mm
Inside margin	5mm
Number of columns	10
Gutter width	2mm
Extras	10 horizontal fields

200% COTTON: NEW T-SHIRT GRAPHICS and
300% COTTON: MORE T-SHIRT GRAPHICS
Design: Agathe Jacquillat and Tomi Vollauschek at Fl@33

These image-based books contain over 1,000 illustrations each. The grid had to be flexible, provide consistency, and make the design process relatively systematic. Designers Agathe Jacquillat and Tomi Vollauschek developed a multicolumn grid with 10 horizontal fields. In *200%* dotted rules form threadlike outlines to frame and connect images and text, foregrounding the grid in a playful way, and making a subtle association with fashion and needlework. The brief for *300%* was to refresh the layout while maintaining the visual identity of the previous title in the series. Jacquillat and Vollauschek chose to exploit the versatility of the grid by introducing diagonals to the layout. The result is a lively reinterpretation of the previously used system.

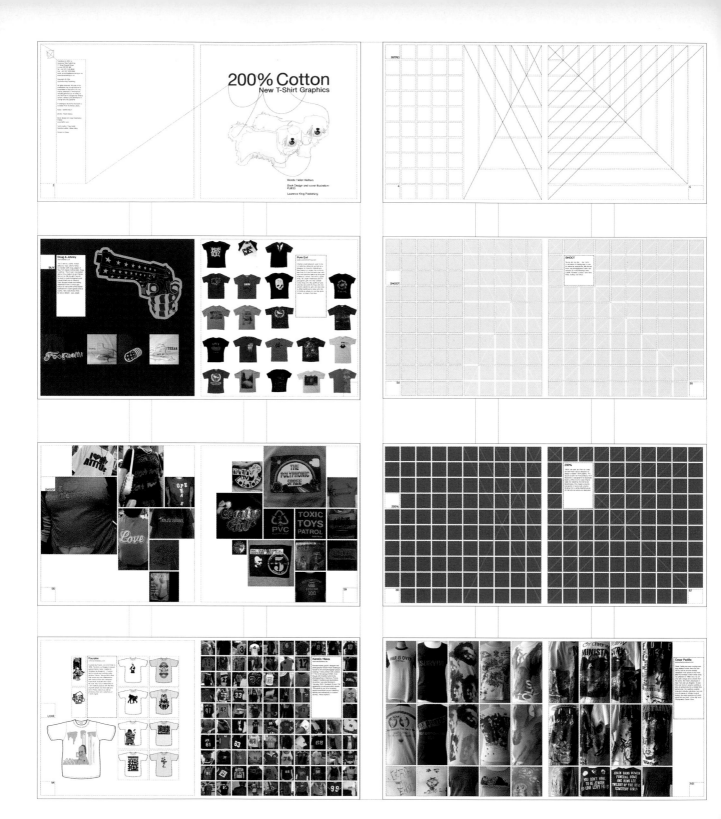

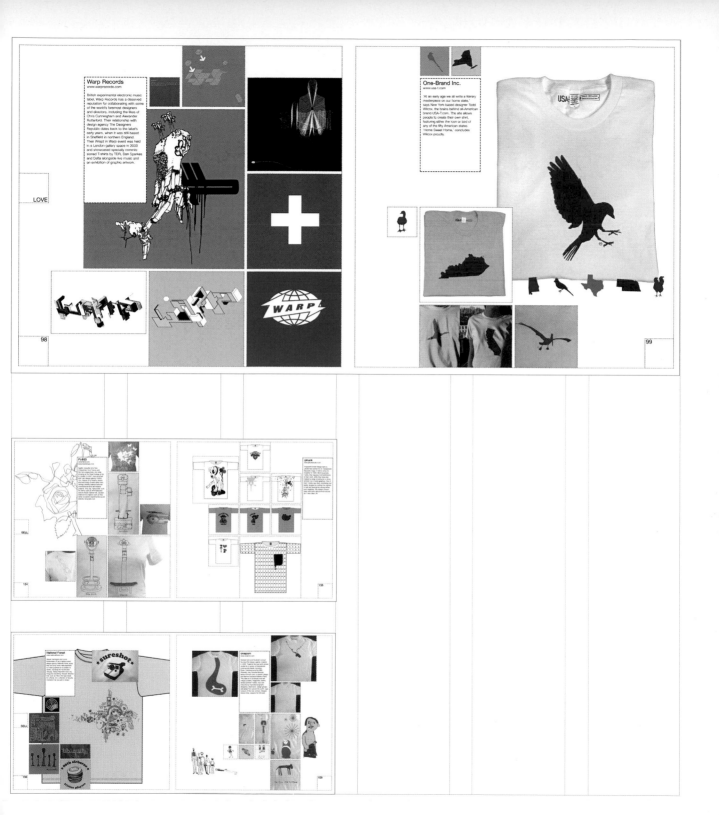

Threadless

Threadless.com

Threadless.com is democracy in progress. The premise is simple: designers upload their ideas for T-shirt graphics to the site. For seven days, viewers can rate the design and, after a week, those with the highest scores go into production. For $200, you can also join their every month club', which sends out a limited-edition shirt every month for a year. 'T-shirts never go out of style, and the good ones only get better with age,' says Jake Nickell.

Designs by Frank Barbara, Jason Baron Nielsen, Thomas Christose, Jess Fink, Dan Gilbert, Glenn Jones, Juc, megafari, Oliver J Moss, Guillermo Marconi, Grace Smith, Ross 2HD.

98 Love
Love 99

Dan Rollman

I KNOW HOW TO
MAKE YOU LAUGH

Worn By

INTRODUCTION

'Take any form you please and repeat it at regular intervals and, as surely as recurrent sounds give rhythm or cadence, whether you want it or not, you have pattern.'

Lewis F. Day

This book is a collection of a number of contemporary surface patterns created between 2000 and 2005 by designers and artists from many different cultures and backgrounds.

The patterns have been achieved by a number of techniques, which include drawing, painting, collage, embroidery, appliqué, hand dyeing and screen printing. Many of the designs have been digitally manipulated. As this was a project facilitated almost entirely by e-mail and digitalized images, this is not surprising. What has been surprising is the range and variety of initiating ideas, as outlined by the artists themselves. These run from 'Mary Poppins Dissected' to 'The Cornish Seascape' to 'Chaos Theory'! I have included the artists' own comments on their inspiration and content wherever possible.

The patterns themselves have been chosen subjectively by me for their perceived qualities of beauty and balance, their use of colour and overall aesthetic appeal. They have been grouped into families following a contemporary understanding of the traditional surface design categories, and I have also arranged the patterns so that they fall in a definite and, I trust, pleasing colour order within each category.

006

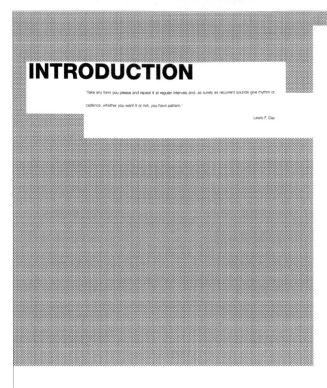

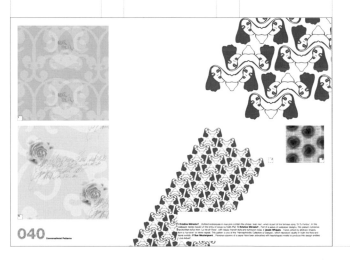

040

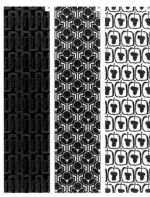

100

INTRODUCTION

Take any form you please and repeat it at regular intervals and, as surely as recurrent sounds give rhythm or cadence, whether you want it or not, you have pattern.

Lewis F. Day

This book is a collection of a number of contemporary surface patterns created between 2000 and 2005 by designers and artists from many different cultures and backgrounds.

The patterns have been achieved by a number of techniques, which include drawing, painting, collage, embroidery, applique, hand dyeing and screen printing. Many of the designs have been digitally manipulated. As this was a project facilitated almost entirely by e-mail and digitalized images, this is not surprising. What has been surprising is the range and variety of initiating ideas, as outlined by the artists themselves. These run from 'Mary Poppins Dissected' to 'The Cornish Seascape' to 'Chaos Theory'! I have included the artists' own comments on their inspiration and content wherever possible.

The patterns themselves have been chosen subjectively by me for their perceived qualities of beauty and balance, their use of colour and overall aesthetic appeal. They have been grouped into families following a contemporary understanding of the traditional surface design categories, and I have also arranged the patterns so that they fall in a definite and, I trust, pleasing colour order within each category.

006

PATTERNS: NEW SURFACE DESIGN

Design: Agathe Jacquillat and Tomi Vollauschek at Fl@33

Coming up with a system that would accommodate examples of elaborate and visually rich pattern making sensitively was a challenge for designers Agathe Jacquillat and Tomi Vollauschek. They had little editorial control over the selection or grouping of the images, which was determined by the author. But, their highly flexible grid allowed them to vary the scale and area used for each example to ensure that the visual relationships between patterns were sympathetic, and potential clashes between designs could be avoided. The page is divided into 12 vertical columns and 17 horizontal fields, with a folio, running foot, and caption zone at the bottom of the page.

GRID SPECIFICATIONS

Page size (trimmed)	170 x 240mm
Top margin	8mm
Bottom margin	16mm
Outside margin	8mm
Inside margin	8mm
Number of columns	12
Gutter width	5mm
Extras	17 horizontal fields

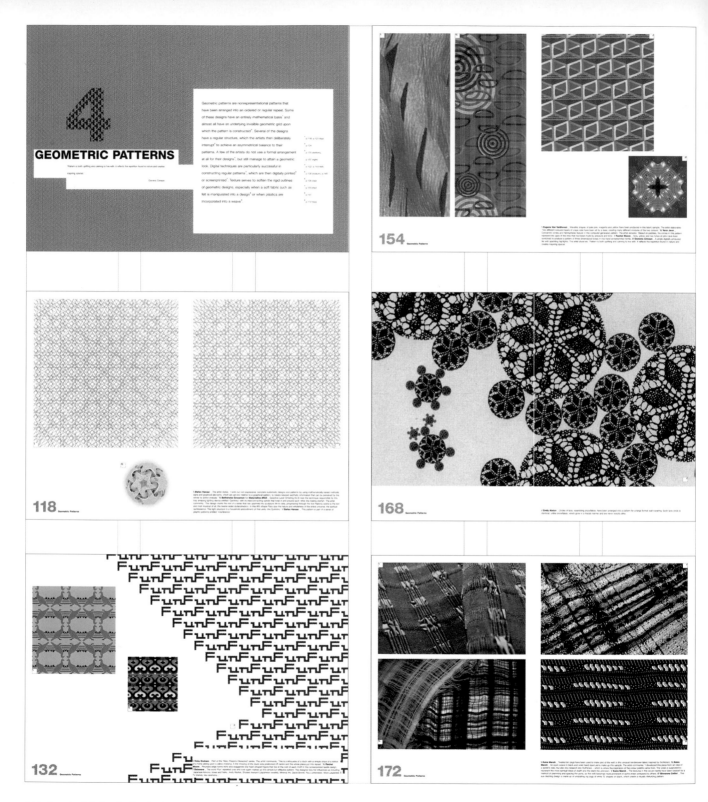

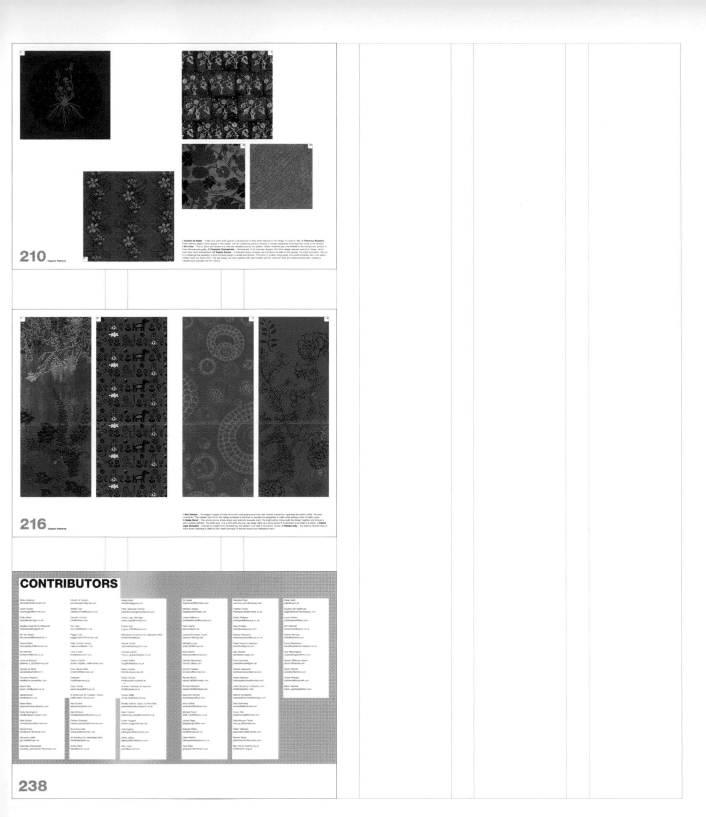

210 Organic Patterns

216 Organic Patterns

CONTRIBUTORS

238

A TALE OF
12 KITCHENS

FAMILY COOKING
IN FOUR COUNTRIES **JAKE TILSON**

"An enchantingly evocative memoir of food and cooking"
CLAUDIA RODEN

SIXTIES POTS AND
SEVENTIES PANS

DON'T GO TO
ANY TROUBLE
BACKSTREET
COUSCOUS

- COUSCOUS
- BROCHETTES
- MERGUEZ
- TARTINES BEURREES
- CROQUE MONSIEUR

A dish that encourages interpretation and invention. I assemble mine with the assimilated memories of smoke-filled Tunisian restaurants in Paris and three memorable meals in a frenzied visit to Morocco in my youth. In Paris they tend towards the separation of the meat from the stew. This becomes an inspiring triad of tastes and texture – soft, dry couscous grains, crisp roast meat accompanied by the wet vegetable stew. Couscous is the name for both the semolina grain and the dish itself. Serve with roasted meat, chicken, lamb, fish or sausages.
Serves 8

5 carrots, sliced in rounds	*spices*
5 courgettes, sliced in rounds	1 stick of cinnamon
3 onions, roughly chopped	1 teaspoon ground cumin
3 large cabbage leaves, shredded	1 teaspoon ground coriander
3 cups chickpeas, precooked or canned	1 teaspoon ground ginger
600ml (1 pint) of chicken stock	1 teaspoon freshly ground cumin seeds
3 cloves of garlic, chopped	10 threads of saffron
3 tablespoons of tomato purée and/or	15 sprigs of fresh coriander, tied in a bunch
1 400g (14oz), can of tomatoes,	15 sprigs of fresh parsley, tied in a bunch
finely mashed	

Vegetable stew – quick method
To achieve a backstreet Parisian-Tunisian style vegetable stew, adopt a nonchalant approach. Put all the ingredients in a large pan, cover with water and simmer for 30 minutes. Done. Serve with couscous grains and roasted or grilled meats.

Variations
You could add harder root vegetables first and softer ones towards the end of cooking for a more consistent bite. Some cooks first fry the spices, onions and garlic until transparent, before adding the remaining ingredients. The key items are carrots, courgettes and chickpeas. Improvise with chicory, shredded cabbage, diced squash or even a stray potato.

Couscous grains
I use a medium wholegrain couscous from our local Iranian store. Barley couscous is also good, with a nutty flavour. I use a quick method for preparing the couscous grains taught to me by a Parisian friend. A medium-grain couscous is easier to cook than fine.
Serves 8

2 cups of medium-grain couscous	1 tablespoon butter
salt	30 sultanas for decoration
saffron (optional)	

Put the couscous grains into a bowl with a few strands of saffron and a little salt. Gently pour boiling water onto the couscous until the water just breaks the surface of the grains, do not mix it. Leave to soak for 20 minutes. Melt a knob of butter in a large pan. The bowl of soaked couscous grains will appear to be a solid mass. With a fork gently plough away the top layer of grains off into the hot buttered pan. Slowly loosen off all of the grains into the pan. Heat through, stirring with a flat-ended wooden spoon for a few minutes. You can cover the pan and reheat later.

Heap the cooked couscous in a pyramid on a warmed round plate and dot a ring of sultanas around the edge.

Accompaniment
Any roasted meat or fish forms the final point of the couscous triad. Country chicken (p 82), *agnello scotaditto* without the sage (p 65). Merguez sausages, grilled fish or fried sardines. A leg of lamb rubbed with cumin, coriander and teaspoon of harissa, then roasted on a bed of outer cabbage leaves sprinkled with caraway seeds. A *couscous royale* in Paris is a mixed platter of chicken, lamb and merguez.

To serve
Transfer the stew to a deep serving bowl with a ladle. Each plate requires a heap of couscous grains, meat and a ladle of vegetable stew. Throughout the meal the couscous grains seem never to diminish on your plate if replenished with enough liquid stew.

Grids: Creative Solutions for Graphic Designers

GRID SPECIFICATIONS

Page size (trimmed)	250 x 196mm
Top margin	11mm
Bottom margin	11mm
Outside margin	15mm
Inside margin	15mm
Number of columns	6
Gutter width	3mm
Extras	N/A

A TALE OF 12 KITCHENS

Design: Jake Tilson at Jake Tilson Studio

As author, designer, photographer, and cook, every aspect of this book is the creation of passionate cook, and artist, Jake Tilson. It provides a distinctive multisensory perspective on seeing and tasting food, from the way it is grown, packaged, and bought, to how it is cooked and remembered. The underlying structure of the book had to support an evocative memoir and a functional cookery book. The grid divides the page into four equal columns and two narrower columns, plus horizontal fields. Although Tilson's recipe layouts are conventional, eclectic combinations of photos, fonts, and ephemera surround them. His goal was to share how much fun food can be, and to produce a guide for his daughter on the significance of cooking and eating in the life of their family.

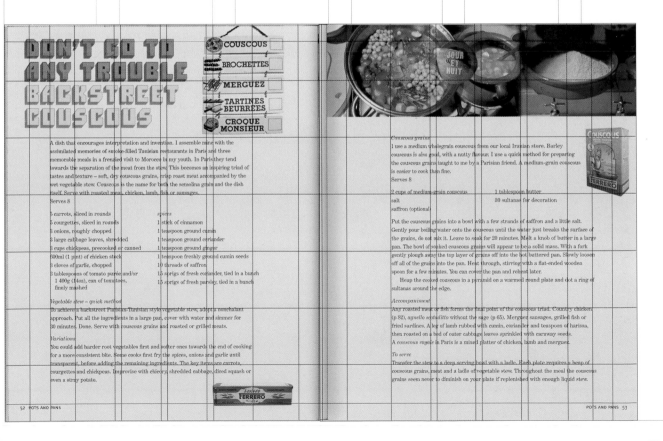

DON'T GO TO ANY TROUBLE BACKSTREET COUSCOUS

- COUSCOUS
- BROCHETTES
- MERGUEZ
- TARTINES BEURRÉES
- CROQUE MONSIEUR

A dish that encourages interpretation and invention. I assemble mine with the assimilated memories of smoke-filled Tunisian restaurants in Paris and three memorable meals in a frenzied visit to Morocco in my youth. In Paris they tend towards the separation of the meat from the stew. This becomes an inspiring triad of tastes and texture – soft, dry couscous grains, crisp roast meat accompanied by the wet vegetable stew. Couscous is the name for both the semolina grain and the dish itself. Serve with roasted meat, chicken, lamb, fish or sausages.

Serves 8

	spices
5 carrots, sliced in rounds	
5 courgettes, sliced in rounds	1 stick of cinnamon
3 onions, roughly chopped	1 teaspoon ground cumin
3 large cabbage leaves, shredded	1 teaspoon ground coriander
3 cups chickpeas, precooked or canned	1 teaspoon ground ginger
600ml (1 pint) of chicken stock	1 teaspoon freshly ground cumin seeds
3 cloves of garlic, chopped	10 threads of saffron
3 tablespoons of tomato purée and/or 1 400g (14oz) can of tomatoes, finely mashed	15 sprigs of fresh coriander, tied in a bunch
	15 sprigs of fresh parsley, tied in a bunch

Vegetable stew – quick method
To achieve a backstreet Parisian-Tunisian style vegetable stew, adopt a nonchalant approach. Put all the ingredients in a large pan, cover with water and simmer for 30 minutes. Done. Serve with couscous grains and roasted or grilled meats.

Variations
You could add harder root vegetables first and softer ones towards the end of cooking for a more consistent bite. Some cooks first fry the spices, onions and garlic until transparent, before adding the remaining ingredients. The key items are carrots, courgettes and chickpeas. Improvise with chicory, shredded cabbage, diced squash or even a stray potato.

Couscous grains
I use a medium wholegrain couscous from our local Iranian store. Barley couscous is also good, with a nutty flavour. I use a quick method for preparing the couscous grains taught to me by a Parisian friend. A medium-grain couscous is easier to cook than fine.
Serves 8

2 cups of medium-grain couscous	1 tablespoon butter
salt	30 sultanas for decoration
saffron (optional)	

Put the couscous grains into a bowl with a few strands of saffron and a little salt. Gently pour boiling water onto the couscous until the water just breaks the surface of the grains, do not mix it. Leave to soak for 20 minutes. Melt a knob of butter in a large pan. The bowl of soaked couscous grains will appear to be a solid mass. With a fork gently plough away the top layer of grains off into the hot buttered pan. Slowly loosen off all of the grains into the pan. Heat through, stirring with a flat-ended wooden spoon for a few minutes. You can cover the pan and reheat later.

Heap the cooked couscous in a pyramid on a warmed round plate and dot a ring of sultanas around the edge.

Accompaniment
Any roasted meat or fish forms the final point of the couscous triad. Country chicken (p 82), *agnello scottaditto* without the sage (p 65). Merguez sausages, grilled fish or fried sardines. A leg of lamb rubbed with cumin, coriander and teaspoon of harissa, then roasted on a bed of outer cabbage leaves sprinkled with caraway seeds. A *couscous royale* in Paris is a mixed platter of chicken, lamb and merguez.

To serve
Transfer the stew to a deep serving bowl with a ladle. Each plate requires a heap of couscous grains, meat and a ladle of vegetable stew. Throughout the meal the couscous grains seem never to diminish on your plate if replenished with enough liquid stew.

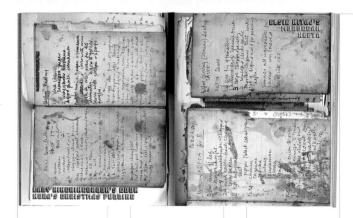

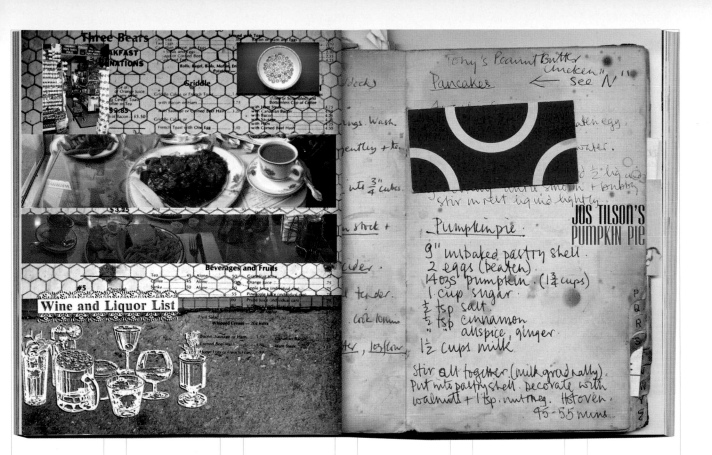

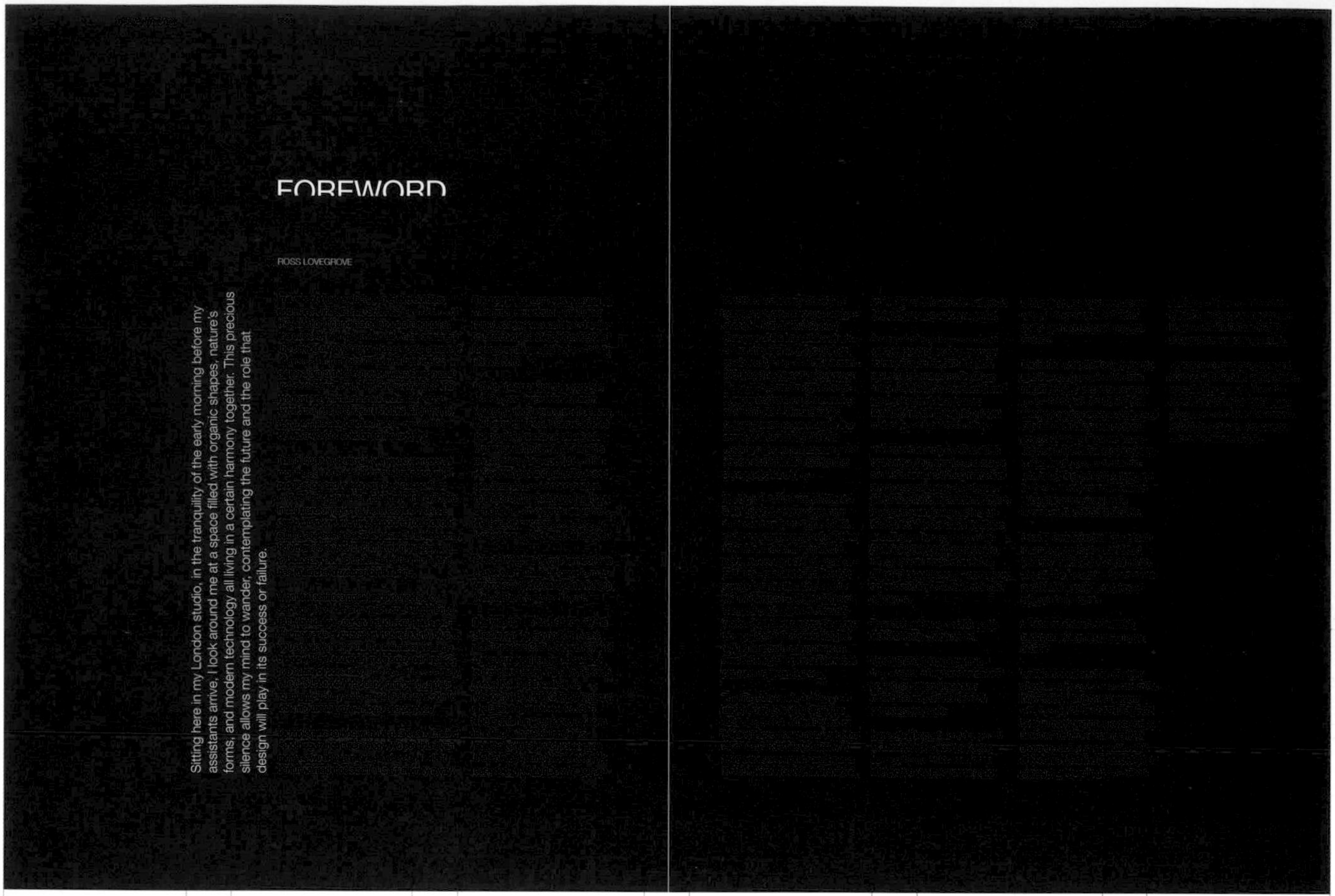

FOREWORD

ROSS LOVEGROVE

Sitting here in my London studio, in the tranquility of the early morning before my assistants arrive, I look around me at a space filled with organic shapes, nature's forms, and modern technology; all living in a certain harmony together. This precious silence allows my mind to wander, contemplating the future and the role that design will play in its success or failure.

DESIGN THIS DAY: 8 DECADES OF INFLUENTIAL DESIGN
Design: Steve Watson, Ben Graham, Jason Gómez, and
Bryan Mamaril at Turnstyle

This limited-edition book was produced to commemorate industrial design company Teague's 80th anniversary. Designers Steve Watson, Ben Graham, Jason Gómez, and Bryan Mamaril wanted the graphic design to reflect the attention to detail characteristic of Teague's design solutions. The typography and navigational devices are clean and systematic, but allow for subtle changes between sections. Reminiscent of some of the complex grids developed by the Swiss

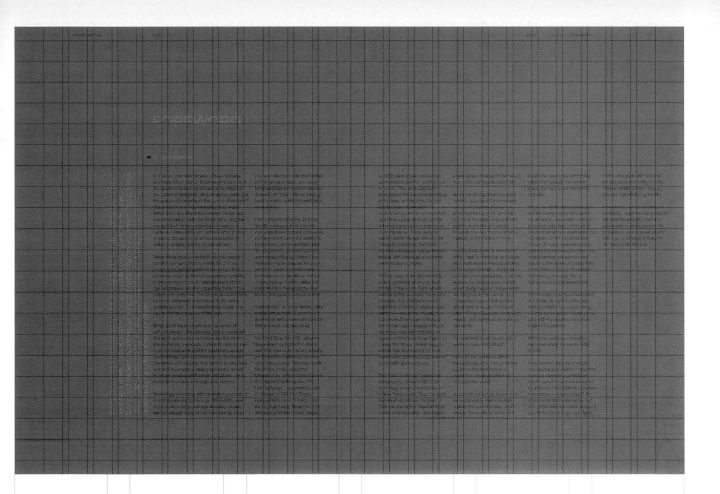

designers of the 1950s and 1960s, their 12-column grid is divided into 20 horizontal fields. The book is not just a showcase of Teague's finished work—it gives context by drawing on their initial ideas and methods of working, as well as showing the work of their design heroes. This provided an opportunity for Turnstyle to vary the visual pace of the book and introduce different paper stocks to make this a tactile as well as a visual experience.

GRID SPECIFICATIONS

Page size (trimmed)	228.6 x 304.8mm
Top margin	9.525mm
Bottom margin	9.525mm
Outside margin	9.525mm
Inside margin	19.05mm
Number of columns	12
Gutter width	4.064mm
Extras	Baseline grid, 0.706mm starting at 9.525mm; 20 horizontal fields

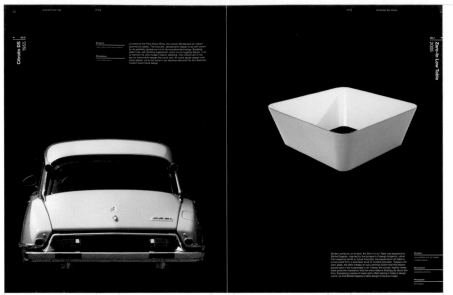

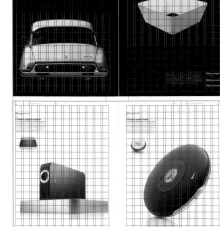

Client

Samsung Electronics

→ 04.1

Portable Digital Projector

The compact and ultra portable projector was designed specifically for the highly mobile professional. Created to fit easily into today's busy schedule—not to mention a small bag or purse—the Samsung Portable Digital Projector is no larger than a digital camera. Utilizing laser diode technology to offer an integrated and seamless display experience, users interact with and control the extremely versatile projector via their mobile phone.

Date	Award	Award
2004	2005 IF	2006 IDEA Silver

Client

Nike

→ 04.2

Portable Sports Audio

Teague worked with Nike's in-house team on all design aspects of this lightweight, rugged, and sophisticated family of products. Designed for the serious athlete, the MP3 Run's wireless features include a distance and speed sensor, as well as skip-free audio and FM radio that keeps athletes in tune with their music and their workout. The complementary MP3 CD's shock-resistant technology, no-look control belt, and strobe light all cater to the athlete who wants an uninterrupted workout experience.

Date
2003

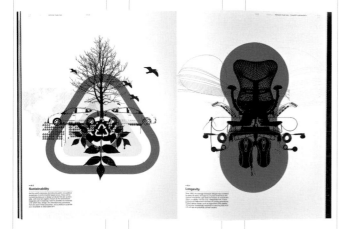

GIAN LORENZO
BERNINI
Apollo and Daphne
1622-1625
marble

1. THE MYTH OF ER

In the tremendous vision of transmigration which closes Plato's *Republic,* the dead are able to choose their fate in their future lives: Socrates describes how a warrior called Er was taken for dead and entered the other world, but came back to life on his funeral pyre; after he had returned from the other world, he described how he saw there, in "a certain demonic place," the souls of Homeric heroes taking on their next existence—in the form of a new daimon. The dead were told, "A demon will not select you, but you will choose a demon. Let him who gets the first lot make the first choice of a life to which he will be bound by necessity."[1] As Er watches the redistribution of lives after death, he recognizes Orpheus who chooses to become a swan, Ajax who singles out the life of a lion, and Agamemnon who decides to become an eagle. The heroes' future metamorphoses in some ways correspond to their past character, sometimes ironically. Atalanta, the swift runner, chooses to become a male athlete, for example; Epeius, who made the Trojan horse, opts to become a female

53

METETA MOMOR PHOHOS IS S

MARINA WArner

I. THE
MYTH
OF ER

In the tremendous vision of transmigration which closes Plato's *Republic,*
the dead are able to choose their fate in their future lives. Socrates describes
how a warrior called Er was taken for dead and entered the other world, but came back
to life on his funeral pyre; after he had returned from the other world, he
described how he saw there, in "a certain demonic place," the souls of Homeric
heroes taking on their next existence—in the form of a new daimon. The
dead were told, "A demon will not select you, but you will choose a demon. Let him
who gets the first lot make the first choice of a life to which he will be bound by necessity."[1] As Er watches the redistribution of lives after death, he recognizes
Orpheus who chooses to become a swan, Ajax who singles out the life of
a lion, and Agamemnon who decides to become an eagle. The heroes' future
metamorphoses in some ways correspond to their past character, sometimes
ironically. Atalanta, the swift runner, chooses to become a male athlete,
for example; Epeius, who made the Trojan horse, opts to become a female

GIAN LORENZO
BERNINI
Apollo and Daphne
1622-1625
marble

GRID SPECIFICATIONS

Page size (trimmed)	152.4 x 203.2mm
Top margin	19.05mm
Bottom margin	12.7mm
Outside margin	19.05mm
Inside margin	12.7mm
Number of columns	9
Gutter width	3.81mm
Extras	N/A

UNEASY NATURE

*Design: Eric Heiman, Amber Reed, and Madhavi Jagdish
at Volume Inc.*

This exhibition catalog was produced for Weatherspoon Art Museum.
The designers explored ideas of mutation by juxtaposing the natural
and the unnatural in their design. They started with the cover, on
which all the images from the show are overlaid digitally to create a
single composite image. The typographic grid uses the golden section,
however, the designers break this grid repeatedly, with various
typographic mutations that often bleed off the pages. The body text
changes from sans serif to serif throughout the essays, and on the
whole, text and image are not integrated. The cover and essay pages
are printed in two colors on uncoated cream stock, while the images
are contained within a full-color section on coated white paper.

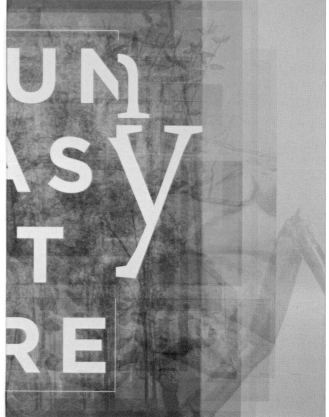

LEE BUL
BRYAN CROCKETT
ROXY PAINE
PATRICIA PICCININI
ALYSON SHOTZ
JENNIFER STEINKAMP

UN
EASY
NAT URE

NEW perceptions
OF nature in
CONtemporary
art.

... I think there
are things
that are real

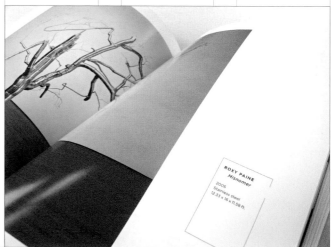

ROXY PAINE
Misnomer

2005
Stainless steel
12.33 × 18 × 11.58 ft.

Grids: Creative Solutions for Graphic Designers

CONTENTS

6 **Introduction** G Stanley Collyer
   Why Compete? G Stanley Collyer

22 **Chapter 1 Government Buildings** G Stanley Collyer
34 Eugene, Oregon Federal Courthouse (1999) John Morris Dixon
40 Canadian Embassy, Berlin (1998) G Stanley Collyer
46 Contra Costa County Government Center (2000) Mark Tortorich
54 Los Angeles Federal Courthouse (2001) Larry Gordon

60 **Chapter 2 Performing Arts Centres** G Stanley Collyer
72 Rensselaer Polytechnic Electronic Media and Performing Arts Center (2001) W Morgan
78 Tempe Visual & Performing Arts Center (2001) Brian Taggart
84 Jyväskylä Music and Arts Centre (1998) William Morgan
88 Miami-Dade Performing Arts Center (1995) Carlos Casuscelli

96 **Chapter 3 Educational Facilities** G Stanley Collyer
106 Lick-Wilmerding High School, San Francisco (2001) Susannah Temko
116 Chicago Prototype Schools (2001) G Stanley Collyer
124 Booker T Washington Arts Magnet School, Dallas (2001) Mark Gunderson AIA
130 IIT McCormick Center, Chicago (1998) Michael Dulin
136 University of South Dakota School of Business (2000) Tom Reasoner
142 School of Architecture, University of New Mexico (2000) Brian Taggart

148 **Chapter 4 Public Libraries** Roger L Schluntz FAIA
158 Salt Lake City Library (2000) Roger L Schluntz FAIA
164 Kansai-Kan National Diet Library (1996) Tony Coscia
170 Brooklyn Public Library (2002) Michael Berk
178 Québec Library, Montréal (2000) William Morgan

184 **Chapter 5 Museums** G Stanley Collyer
194 Modern Art Museum of Fort Worth (1997) George Wright
200 Palos Verdes Art Center (2000) Larry Gordon
206 Nam June Paik Museum (2003) G Stanley Collyer

212 **Chapter 6 Housing** Robert G Shibley AIA, AICP
220 Chicago Housing Authority (2001) Rosemarie Buchanan
226 Europan (1993) Lucy Bullivard
232 Sustainable Housing, Lystrup, Århus, Denmark (2003) G Stanley Collyer

238 Appendix – Competitions by Country
246 Bibliography
247 Photo Credits
248 Acknowledgements
249 Contributors
250 Index

4

5

IIT McCormick Center, Chicago (1998)

Michael Dulin

Government Buildings

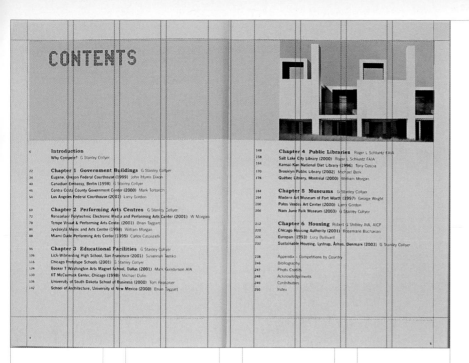

CONTENTS

6   **Introduction**
Why Compete? G Stanley Collyer

22   **Chapter 1 Government Buildings** G Stanley Collyer
34   Eugene, Oregon Federal Courthouse (1999) John Morris Dixon
40   Canadian Embassy, Berlin (1998) G Stanley Collyer
46   Contra Costa County Government Center (2000) Mark Tortorich
54   Los Angeles Federal Courthouse (2003) Larry Gordon

60   **Chapter 2 Performing Arts Centres** G Stanley Collyer
72   Rensselaer Polytechnic Electronic Media and Performing Arts Center (2001) W Morgan
78   Tempe Visual & Performing Arts Center (2001) Brian Taggart
84   Jyväskylä Music and Arts Centre (1998) William Morgan
88   Miami-Dade Performing Arts Center (1995) Carlos Casuscelli

96   **Chapter 3 Educational Facilities** G Stanley Collyer
106   Lick-Wilmerding High School, San Francisco (2001) Susannah Temko
116   Chicago Prototype Schools (2001) G Stanley Collyer
124   Booker T Washington Arts Magnet School, Dallas (2001) Mark Gunderson AIA
130   IIT McCormick Center, Chicago (1998) Michael Dulin
136   University of South Dakota School of Business (2000) Tom Reasoner
142   School of Architecture, University of New Mexico (2000) Brian Taggart

148   **Chapter 4 Public Libraries** Roger L Schluntz FAIA
158   Salt Lake City Library (2000) Roger L Schluntz FAIA
164   Kansai-Kan National Diet Library (1996) Tony Coscia
170   Brooklyn Public Library (2002) Michael Berk
178   Québec Library, Montréal (2000) William Morgan

184   **Chapter 5 Museums** G Stanley Collyer
194   Modern Art Museum of Fort Worth (1997) George Wright
200   Palos Verdes Art Center (2000) Larry Gordon
206   Nam June Paik Museum (2003) G Stanley Collyer

212   **Chapter 6 Housing** Robert G Shibley AIA, AICP
220   Chicago Housing Authority (2001) Rosemarie Buchanan
226   Europan (1993) Lucy Bullivant
232   Sustainable Housing, Lystrup, Århus, Denmark (2003) G Stanley Collyer

238   Appendix - Competitions by Country
246   Bibliography
247   Photo Credits
248   Acknowledgements
249   Contributors
250   Index

GRID SPECIFICATIONS

Page size (trimmed)	240 x 164mm
Top margin	15mm
Bottom margin	22mm
Outside margin	12mm
Inside margin	17mm
Number of columns	1, 2, or 4
Gutter width	4mm
Extras	N/A

AP ARCHITECTURE IN PRACTICE
Design: Christian Küsters at CHK Design

Christian Küsters developed an accessible and user-friendly system for this series of practice-based architectural books. The design is based on a single matrix that forms the basis of the logotype, and is the inspiration for the headline font, as well as the grid system of the book. The grid defines areas for a large heading zone at the top, one wide column and related information to the left, or two columns of continuous text. Küsters wanted the books to feel like handbooks, and designed the font Matrix specifically for this series. His choice of secondary fonts included New Gothic, because it is spatially economical and architectural in feel, contrasted with Bookman Old Style.

Identities

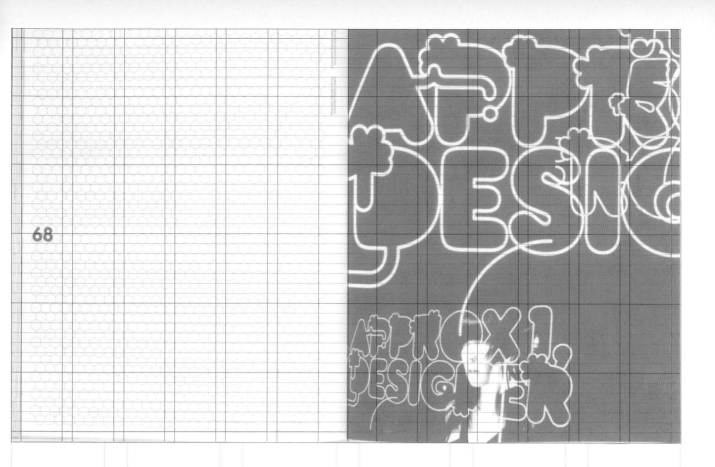

68

GRID SPECIFICATIONS

Page size (trimmed)	210 x 170mm
Top margin	5mm
Bottom margin	5mm
Outside margin	5mm
Inside margin	15mm
Number of columns	6
Gutter width	5mm
Extras	Baseline grid 5mm; 6 horizontal fields

365 PAGES

Design: BB/Saunders

Every week, members of design and branding consultancy
BB/Saunders produce a diary for inclusion on its website.
The brief is open; it might be a map of somebody's last seven days
or a manifesto calling to save the world. The initial idea behind *365
Pages* was to catalog these and create a journal of diaries. Based
on the assumption that designers love to doodle in sketchbooks,
BB/Saunders went on to create a book that included inventive and
unusual multicolumn and field-based grids as backgrounds to the
pages—the objective was to encourage readers to record their own
daily experiences, observations, or thoughts. Using its in-house
technical drafting grids as a starting point, 12 new grids were
created for this book.

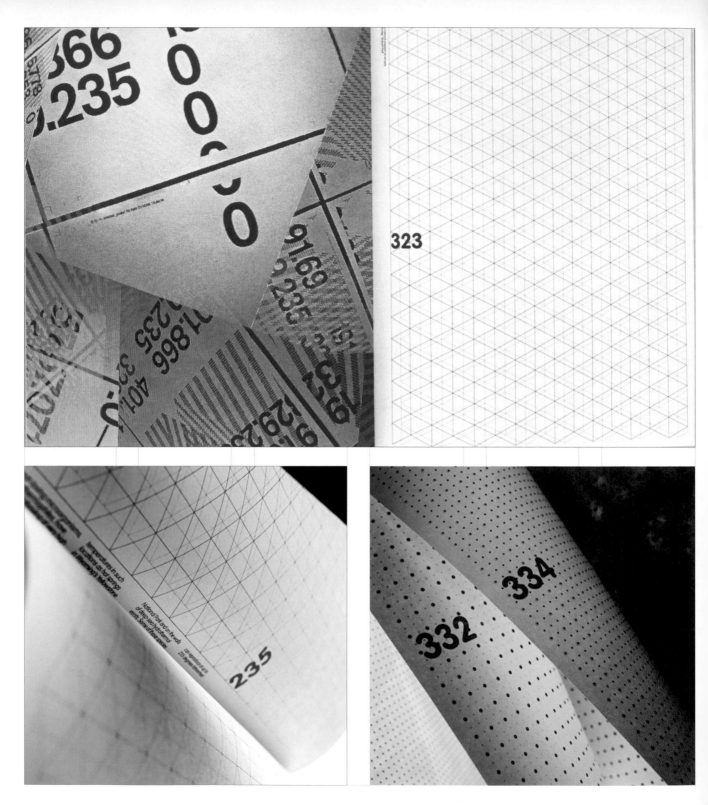

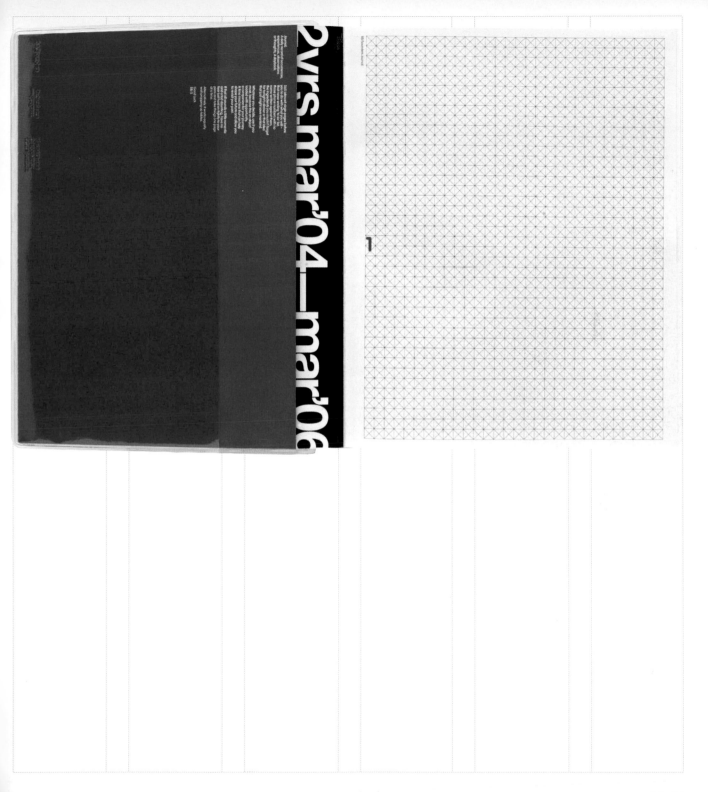

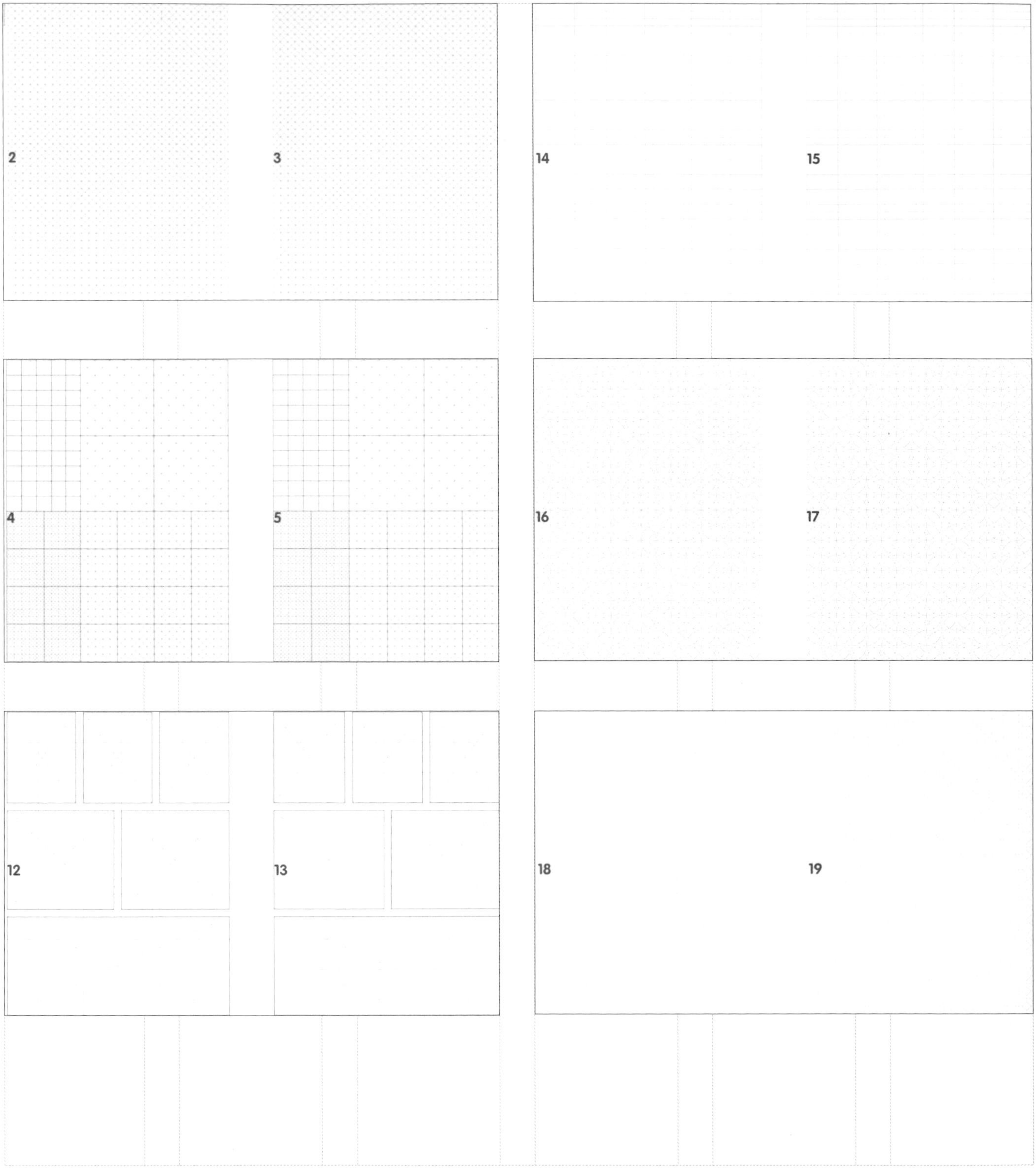

2   3

14   15

4   5

16   17

12   13

18   19

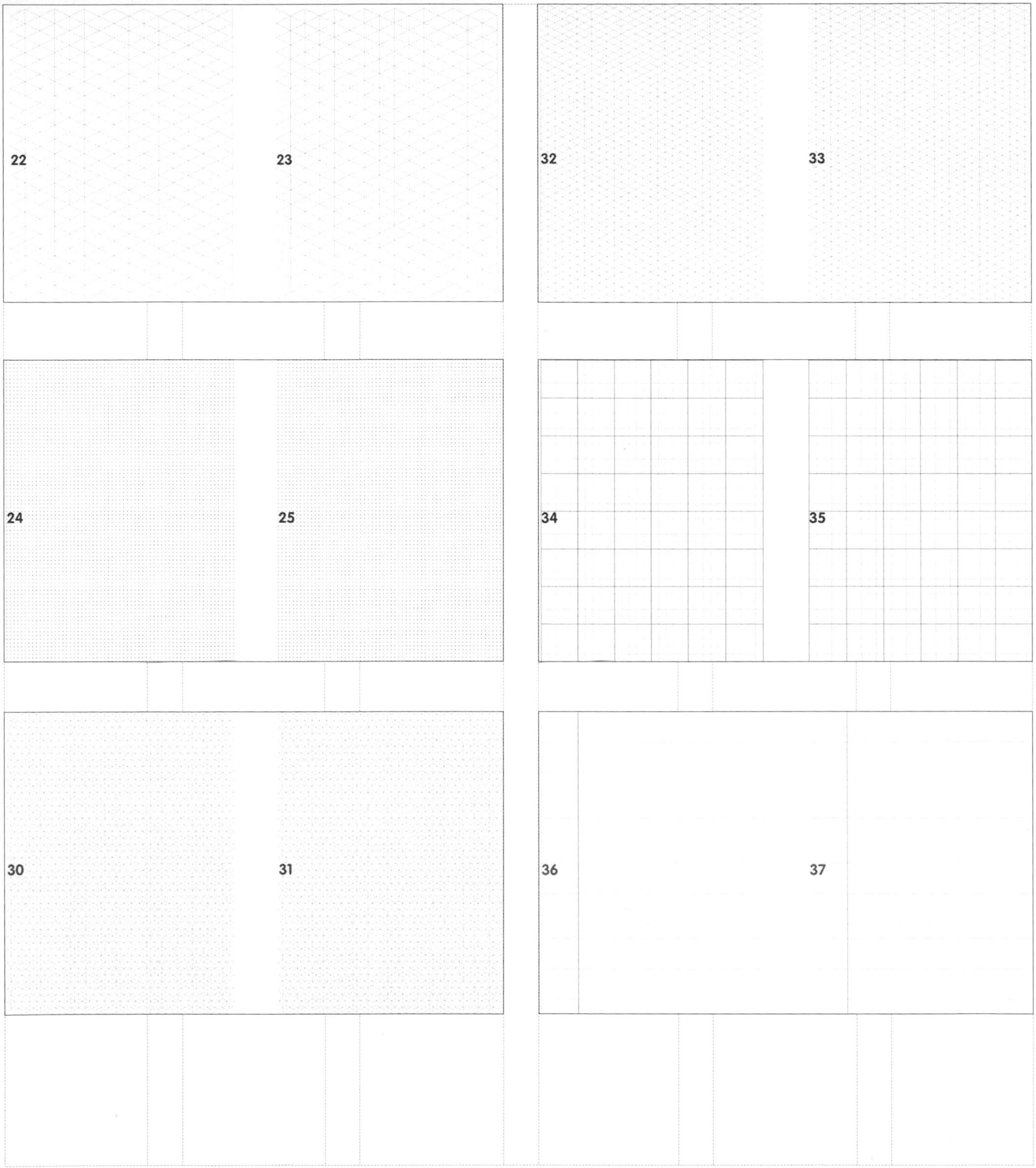

22 23

32 33

24 25

34 35

30 31

36 37

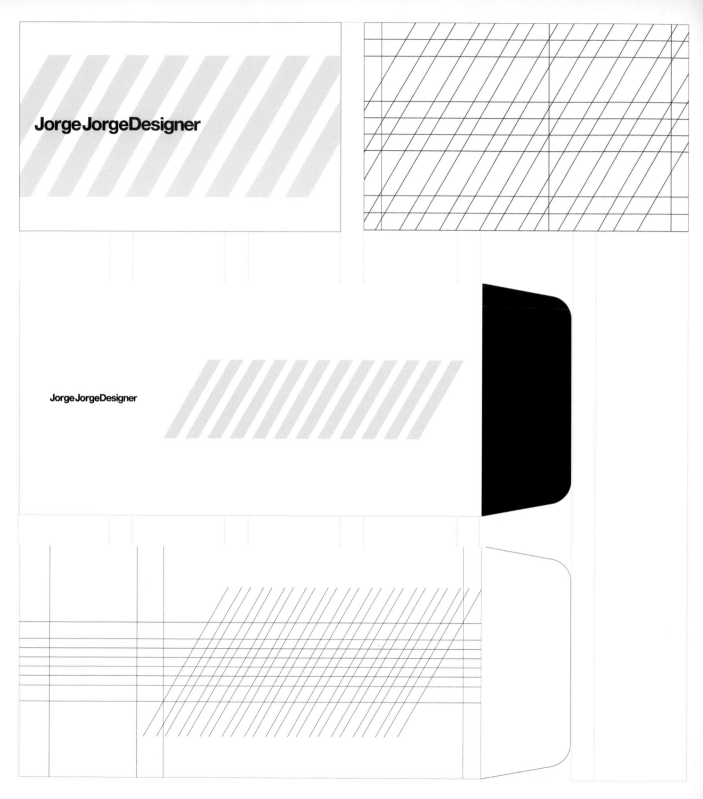

JORGE JORGE DESIGN IDENTITY

Design: Jorge Jorge at Jorge Jorge Design

Jorge Jorge's aim was to create a simple and contemporary identity that would work across a range of graphic applications and formats, and communicate his personality and potential to clients. He achieved this through economic means; the diagonal rules and use of limited color distinguish a considered and minimal layout. Although grids are used most prevalently in multipage documents, they can also be used very effectively across a range of related single-page items. Here Jorge Jorge's grid ensures consistency. It determines hanging heights and alignments across each element of the stationery.

For: Dr. João Soares
Company: Brand Y
Fax nº: 225 876 987
Subject: Something

From: Jorge Jorge
Pages: 1/2
Date: 22/02/07
Reply to: JorgeJorge / 225 899 645

Jorge Jorge Designer

Porto, 14 Janeiro 2007

Olá João Soares!

Lorem ipsum dolor sit amet, consectetuer adipiscing elit, sed diam nonummy nibh euismod tincidunt ut laoreet dolore magna aliquam erat volutpat. Ut wisi enim ad minim veniam, quis nostrud exerci tation ullamcorper suscipit lobortis nisl ut aliquip ex ea commodo consequat. Duis autem vel eum iriure dolor in hendrerit in vulputate velit esse molestie consequat, vel illum dolore eu feugiat nulla facilisis at vero eros et accumsan et iusto odio dignissim qui blandit praesent luptatum zzril delenit augue duis dolore te feugait nulla facilisi. Lorem ipsum dolor sit amet, consectetuer adipiscing elit, sed diam nonummy nibh euismod tincidunt ut laoreet dolore magna aliquam erat volutpat. Ut wisi enim ad minim veniam, quis nostrud exerci tation ullamcorper suscipit lobortis nisl ut aliquip ex ea commodo consequat.

Duis autem vel eum iriure dolor in hendrerit in vulputate velit esse molestie consequat, vel illum dolore eu feugiat nulla facilisis at vero eros et accumsan et iusto odio dignissim qui blandit praesent luptatum zzril delenit augue duis dolore te feugait nulla facilisi. Nam liber tempor cum soluta nobis eleifend option congue nihil imperdiet doming id quod mazim placerat facer possim assum. Lorem ipsum dolor sit amet, consectetuer adipiscing elit, sed diam nonummy nibh euismod tincidunt ut laoreet dolore magna aliquam erat volut

Aguardo contacto seu!
Cumprimentos,

Jorge Jorge

+351 934 201 420
mail@jorgejorge.com
www.jorgejorge.com

Internal Memo   Subject: New Briefing

Jorge Jorge Designer

Subject 01

Lorem ipsum dolor sit amet, consectetuer adipiscing elit, sed diam nonummy nibh euismod tincidunt ut laoreet dolore magna aliquam erat volutpat. Ut wisi enim ad minim veniam, quis nostrud exerci tation ullamcorper suscipit lobortis nisl ut aliquip ex ea commodo consequat. Duis autem vel eum iriure dolor in hendrerit in vulputate velit esse molestie consequat, vel illum dolore eu feugiat nulla facilisis at vero eros et accumsan et iusto odio dignissim qui blandit praesent luptatum zzril delenit augue duis dolore te feugait nulla facilisi. Lorem ipsum dolor sit amet, consectetuer adipiscing elit, sed diam nonummy nibh euismod tincidunt ut laoreet dolore magna aliquam erat volutpat. Ut wisi enim ad minim veniam, quis nostrud exerci tation ullamcorper suscipit lobortis nisl ut aliquip ex ea commodo consequat.

Subject 02

Duis autem vel eum iriure dolor in hendrerit in vulputate velit esse molestie consequat, vel illum dolore eu feugiat nulla facilisis at vero eros et accumsan et iusto odio dignissim qui blandit praesent luptatum zzril delenit augue duis dolore te feugait nulla facilisi. Nam liber tempor cum soluta nobis eleifend option congue nihil imperdiet doming id quod mazim placerat facer possim assum. Lorem ipsum dolor sit amet, consectetuer adipiscing elit, sed diam nonummy nibh euismod tincidunt ut laoreet dolore magna aliquam erat volut

+351 934 201 420
mail@jorgejorge.com
www.jorgejorge.com

Subject:

Jorge Jorge Designer

Porto, 14 Janeiro 2007

Olá João Soares!

Lorem ipsum dolor sit amet, consectetuer adipiscing elit, sed diam nonummy nibh euismod tincidunt ut laoreet dolore magna aliquam erat volutpat. Ut wisi enim ad minim veniam, quis nostrud exerci tation ullamcorper suscipit lobortis nisl ut aliquip ex ea commodo consequat. Duis autem vel eum iriure dolor in hendrerit in vulputate velit esse molestie consequat, vel illum dolore eu feugiat nulla facilisis at vero eros et accumsan et iusto odio dignissim qui blandit praesent luptatum zzril delenit augue duis dolore te feugait nulla facilisi. Lorem ipsum dolor sit amet, consectetuer adipiscing elit, sed diam nonummy nibh euismod tincidunt ut laoreet dolore magna aliquam erat volutpat. Ut wisi enim ad minim veniam, quis nostrud exerci tation ullamcorper suscipit lobortis nisl ut aliquip ex ea commodo consequat.

Duis autem vel eum iriure dolor in hendrerit in vulputate velit esse molestie consequat, vel illum dolore eu feugiat nulla facilisis at vero eros et accumsan et iusto odio dignissim qui blandit praesent luptatum zzril delenit augue duis dolore te feugait nulla facilisi. Nam liber tempor cum soluta nobis eleifend option congue nihil imperdiet doming id quod mazim placerat facer possim assum. Lorem ipsum dolor sit amet, consectetuer adipiscing elit, sed diam nonummy nibh euismod tincidunt ut laoreet dolore magna aliquam erat volut

Aguardo contacto seu!
Cumprimentos,

Jorge Jorge

+351 934 201 420
mail@jorgejorge.com
www.jorgejorge.com

Subject:

JorgeJorge**Designer**

Porto, 14 Janeiro 2007

Olá João Soares!
Lorem ipsum dolor sit amet, consectetuer adipiscing elit, sed diam nonummy nibh euismod tincidunt ut laoreet dolore magna aliquam erat volutpat. Ut wisi enim ad minim veniam, quis nostrud exerci tation ullamcorper suscipit lobortis nisl ut aliquip ex ea commodo consequat. Duis autem vel eum iriure dolor in hendrerit in vulputate velit esse molestie consequat, vel illum dolore eu feugiat nulla facilisis at vero eros et accumsan et iusto odio dignissim qui blandit praesent luptatum zzril delenit augue duis dolore te feugait nulla facilisi. Lorem ipsum dolor sit amet, consectetuer adipiscing elit, sed diam nonummy nibh euismod tincidunt ut laoreet dolore magna aliquam erat volutpat. Ut wisi enim ad minim veniam, quis nostrud exerci tation ullamcorper suscipit lobortis nisl ut aliquip ex ea commodo consequat.
Duis autem vel eum iriure dolor in hendrerit in vulputate velit esse molestie consequat, vel illum dolore eu feugiat nulla facilisis at vero eros et accumsan et iusto odio dignissim qui blandit praesent luptatum zzril delenit augue duis dolore te feugait nulla facilisi. Nam liber tempor cum soluta nobis eleifend option congue nihil imperdiet doming id quod mazim placerat facer possim assum. Lorem ipsum dolor sit amet, consectetuer adipiscing elit, sed diam nonummy nibh euismod tincidunt ut laoreet dolore magna aliquam erat volut

Aguardo contacto seu!
Cumprimentos,

Jorge Jorge

+351 934 201 420
mail@jorgejorge.com
www.jorgejorge.com

GRID SPECIFICATIONS

Page size (trimmed)	Card: 850 x 550mm
	Letterhead: 210 x 297mm
	Envelope: 110 x 220mm
Top margin	Card: 90mm
	Letterhead: 270mm
	Envelope: 350mm
Bottom margin	Card: 90mm
	Letterhead: 250mm
	Envelope: 350mm
Outside margin	Card: 9mm
	Letterhead: 27mm
	Envelope: 35mm
Inside margin	Card: 9mm
	Letterhead: 25mm
	Envelope: 35mm
Number of columns	Card: 4
	Letterhead: 5
	Envelope: 5
Gutter width	N/A
Extras	Card and envelope: 9 horizontal fields
	Letterhead: 20 horizontal fields

Lund+Slaatto
ARKITEKTER

Besøk Drammensveien 145 A
Post Pb 69 Skøyen, 0212 Oslo

Espen Pedersen
Sivilarkitekt MNLA / Partner

Besøk Drammensveien 145 A
Post Pb 69 Skøyen, 0212 Oslo

Dir +47 22 12 29 15
Mob +47 90 72 24 25
Email pedersen@lsa.no

Tel +47 22 12 29 00
Fax +47 22 12 29 99
Web www.lsa.no

Lund+Slaatto
ARKITEKTER

Espen Pedersen
Sivilarkitekt MNLA / Partner

Besøk Drammensveien 145 A
Post Pb 69 Skøyen, 0212 Oslo

Dir +47 22 12 29 15
Mob +47 90 72 24 25
Email pedersen@lsa.no

Tel +47 22 12 29 00
Fax +47 22 12 29 99
Web www.lsa.no

Lund+Slaatto
ARKITEKTER

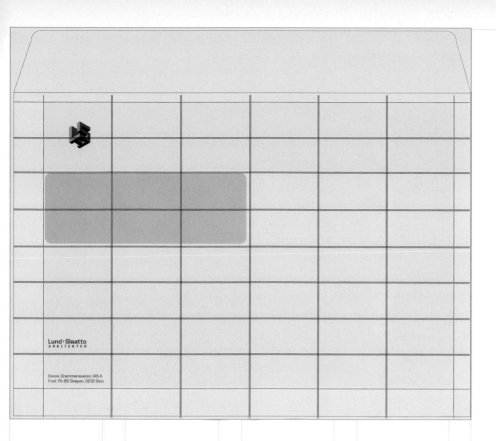

GRID SPECIFICATIONS

Page size (trimmed)	Envelope: 228 x 161mm
	Card: 45.5 x 89mm
Top margin	Envelope: 4mm/Card: 0.5mm
Bottom margin	Envelope: 14mm/Card: 0.5mm
Outside margin	Envelope: 15mm/Card: 0.5mm
Inside margin	Envelope: 8mm/Card: 0.5mm
Number of columns	Envelope: 6/Card: 3
Gutter width	Envelope: 0.5mm/Card: 0.5mm
Extras	Base unit—landscape rectangle with a ratio of 2:1; baseline grid, 7pt; Envelope: 9 horizontal fields/ Card: 3 horizontal fields

LUND+SLAATTO STATIONERY

Design: Karl Martin Saetren at Mission Design

Mission Design developed this identity for leading Norwegian architects Lund+Slaatto. The pared down, clean design reflects the attention to detail and architectural style for which the client is known. The layout is based on a grid using fields that have a ratio of 2:1. To ensure consistency between small items, such as business cards, and larger pieces of print, this proportion is used in all the grids, although the overall size of each field does change. For large items, more fields are added to the overall grid. In this way the grid works across a range of scales and formats.

DAMIAN HEINISCH PHOTOGRAPHER

01 —

02 —

DAMIAN MICHAL HEINISCH
GRENSEVEIEN 11F
0571 OSLO, NORWAY
TLF +47 45 02 43 71
CONTACT@DAMIANHEINISCH.COM
WWW.DAMIAN HEINISCH
ORG.NR. 983 587 305

Grids: Creative Solutions for Graphic Designers

01 —

02 —

GRID SPECIFICATIONS

Page size (trimmed)	210 x 297mm
Top margin	7.5mm
Bottom margin	8mm
Outside margin	N/A
Inside margin	N/A
Number of columns	34
Gutter width	1mm
Extras	Baseline grid, 24pt

DAMIAN HEINISCH STATIONERY

Design: Karl Martin Saetren at Mission Design

Most grids need both horizontal and vertical subdivisions, but this identity, for photographer Damian Heinisch, uses just a series of horizontal stripes that relate to the body height of the type. The smallest type equates to this unit of measurement and fits within the height of one of the grid's units, while the larger type fits within two. The muted color palette and strict systematic design create a distinctive look, while the dark and controlled atmosphere the design exudes echoes the stark and graphic photographs of the client.

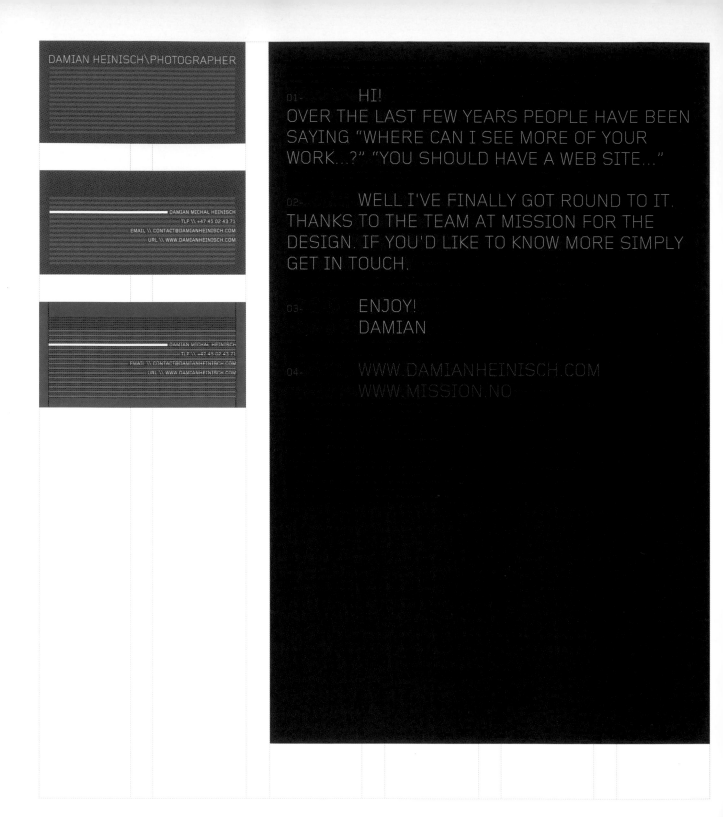

DAMIAN HEINISCH\PHOTOGRAPHER

DAMIAN MICHAL HEINISCH
TLF \\ +47 45 02 43 71
EMAIL \\ CONTACT@DAMIANHEINISCH.COM
URL \\ WWW.DAMIANHEINISCH.COM

DAMIAN MICHAL HEINISCH
TLF \\ +47 45 02 43 71
EMAIL \\ CONTACT@DAMIANHEINISCH.COM
URL \\ WWW.DAMIANHEINISCH.COM

01-   HI!
OVER THE LAST FEW YEARS PEOPLE HAVE BEEN
SAYING "WHERE CAN I SEE MORE OF YOUR
WORK...?" "YOU SHOULD HAVE A WEB SITE..."

02-   WELL I'VE FINALLY GOT ROUND TO IT.
THANKS TO THE TEAM AT MISSION FOR THE
DESIGN. IF YOU'D LIKE TO KNOW MORE SIMPLY
GET IN TOUCH.

03-   ENJOY!
DAMIAN

04-   WWW.DAMIANHEINISCH.COM
WWW.MISSION.NO

HI!
OVER THE LAST FEW YEARS PEOPLE HAVE BEEN
SAYING "WHERE CAN I SEE MORE OF YOUR
WORK...?" "YOU SHOULD HAVE A WEB SITE..."

WELL I'VE FINALLY GOT ROUND TO IT.
THANKS TO THE TEAM AT MISSION FOR THE
DESIGN. IF YOU'D LIKE TO KNOW MORE SIMPLY
GET IN TOUCH.

ENJOY!
DAMIAN

WWW.DAMIANHEINISCH.COM
WWW.MISSION.NO

GRID SPECIFICATIONS

Page size (trimmed)	176.4 x 282.2mm
Top margin	8.8mm
Bottom margin	91.72mm
Outside margin	7.05mm
Inside margin	7.05mm
Number of columns	1
Gutter width	N/A
Extras	Baseline grid, 24pt; 460 horizontal rows, 1.4mm apart

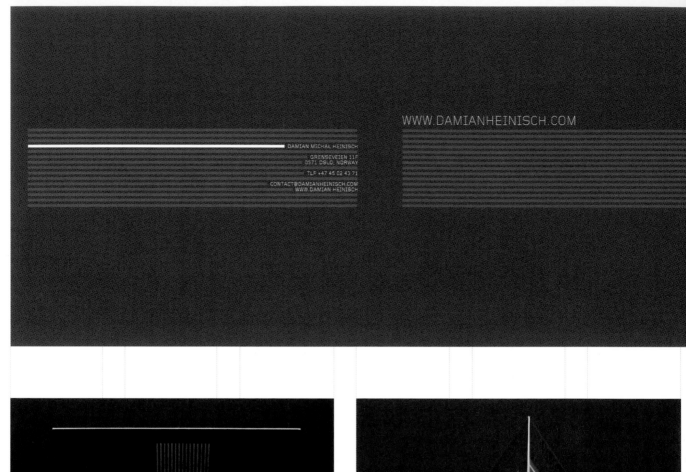

WWW.DAMIANHEINISCH.COM

DAMIAN MICHAL HEINISCH
GRENSEVEIEN 11F
0571 OSLO, NORWAY
TLF +47 45 02 43 71
CONTACT@DAMIANHEINISCH.COM
WWW.DAMIAN HEINISCH

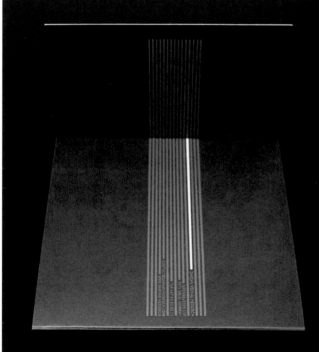

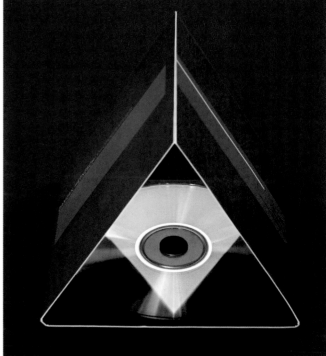

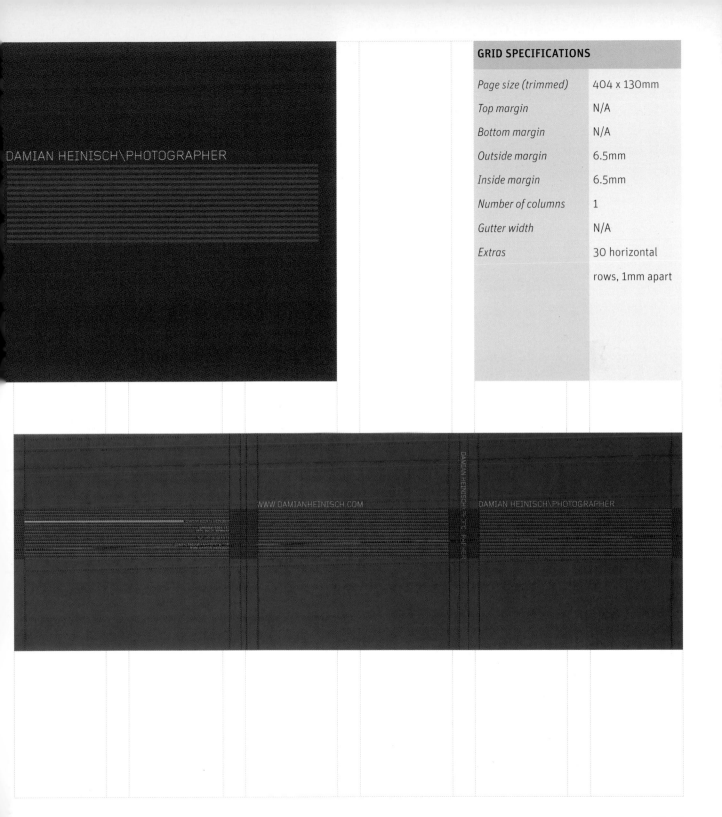

DAMIAN HEINISCH\PHOTOGRAPHER

GRID SPECIFICATIONS

Page size (trimmed)	404 x 130mm
Top margin	N/A
Bottom margin	N/A
Outside margin	6.5mm
Inside margin	6.5mm
Number of columns	1
Gutter width	N/A
Extras	30 horizontal rows, 1mm apart

WWW.DAMIANHEINISCH.COM

DAMIAN HEINISCH\PHOTOGRAPHER

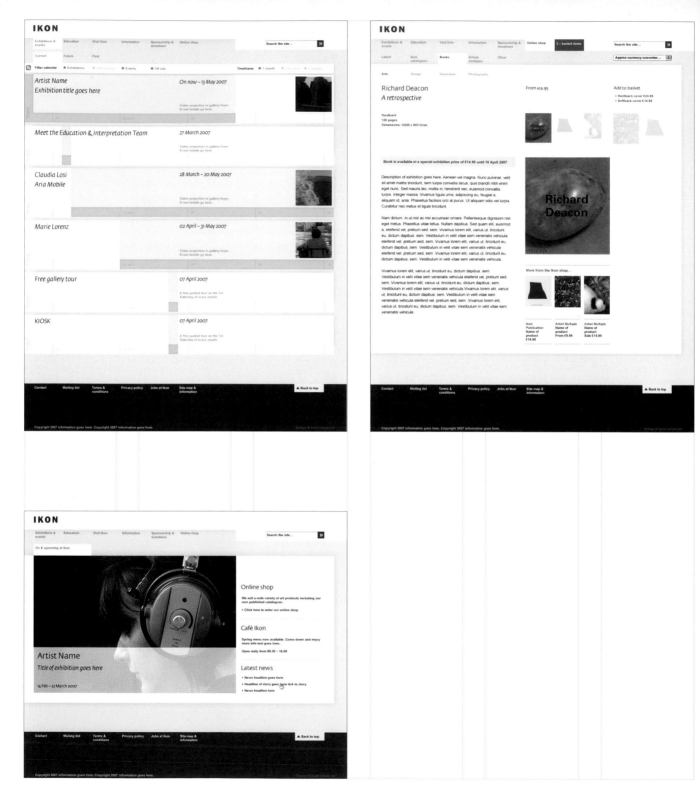

Grids: Creative Solutions for Graphic Designers

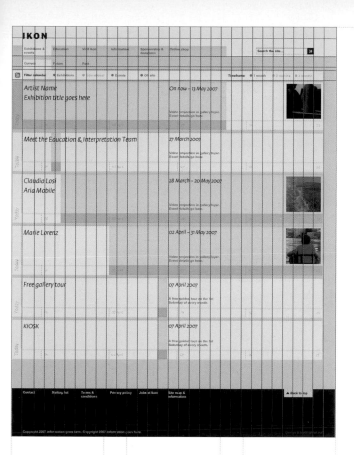

IKON GALLERY WEBSITE

Design: Dom Murphy at TAK!

Although the unit of measurement is different, grids are as relevant to web design as they are to print. The grid for this redesign of the Ikon Gallery website is based around its events calendar and monthly overview. The page is divided into 30-pixel units. This grid determines the position of all elements of the design, from navigation to the placement of information. The grid is most apparent on the events page where the area on the left represents "today," and each block represents a subsequent day. The blue/green panels show the time frame of events over the coming month, and therefore change each day.

GRID SPECIFICATIONS

Page size (trimmed)	270.933 x 361.244mm
Top margin	10.583mm
Bottom margin	10.583mm
Outside margin	10.583mm
Inside margin	10.583mm
Number of columns	15
Gutter width	8.5mm
Extras	4 horizontal fields

Magazines, newspapers & newsletters

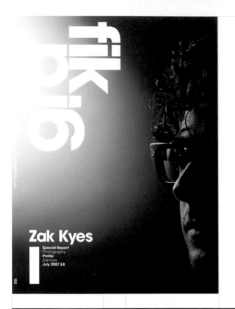

fIK 16

Zak Kyes

Special Report
Photography
Profile
Zak Kyes
July 2007 £8

22
Talent

23
Talent

DONT PANIC

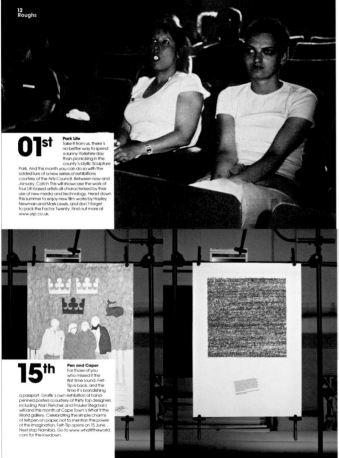

12
Roughs

13
Roughs

01st **Park Life**
Take it from us, there's
no better way to spend
a sunny Yorkshire day
than picnicking in the
county's idyllic Sculpture
Park. And this month you can do so with the
added lure of a new series of exhibitions
courtesy of the Arts Council. Between now and
January, Catch This will showcase the work of
four UK-based artists all characterised by their
use of new media and technology. Head down
this summer to enjoy new film works by Hayley
Newman and Mark Lewis, and don't forget
to pack the Factor Twenty. Find out more at
www.ysp.co.uk.

PRINT RUN
FOR CHARITY
NO. 1046854

PRINT RUN:
10/05/07
PRIVATE:
07/06/07
DISPLAY:

design
makes me sick
design
makes me better
design
makes me
complete.

08th **Picture of Health**
Does design make you
sick? Or, perhaps, is it
the only thing worth
getting up for in the
morning? See how
a selection of the world's top designers and
studios responded to the conundrum of
design's health-giving properties thanks to
a new poster exhibition at London's Kemistry
Gallery this month. Print Run will feature twenty
A1 screenprinted creations from the likes of
Experimental Jetset, Spin and North—and
what's more, all entries will be on sale, with
proceeds going to the Roy Castle Lung
Cancer Foundation. Healthy consciences
all round. Check out www.print-run.org
for further information.

15th **Pen and Caper**
For those of you
who missed it the
first time round, Felt-
Tip is back, and this
time it's brandishing
a passport. Grafik's own exhibition of hand-
penned posters (courtesy of thirty top designers
including Alan Fletcher and Frauke Stegman)
will land this month at Cape Town's What If the
World gallery. Celebrating the simple charms
of felt pen on paper, not to mention the power
of the imagination, Felt-Tip opens on 15 June.
Next stop Namibia. Go to www.whatiftheworld.
com for the lowdown.

15th **Great Expectations**
It's been quite some
time since the
legendary Great
Exhibition of 1851.
This summer, however,
prepare to be transported back in time as
the Royal College of Art stages its own version
to celebrate 150 years at its current South
Kensington location. Bringing together all of
its graduate shows for the very first time, the
RCA will erect an enormous tent in Kensington
Gardens alongside a simultaneous exhibition
at the College Galleries. With the work of
over 400 students on display, they'll certainly
be giving Prince Albert a run for his money.
Full details are available at www.rca.ac.uk.

Grids: Creative Solutions for Graphic Designers

GRID SPECIFICATIONS

Page size (trimmed)	225 x 311mm
Top margin	7mm
Bottom margin	11mm
Outside margin	11mm
Inside margin	20mm
Number of columns	12
Gutter width	2.5mm
Extras	N/A

GRAFIK
Design: SEA

Designing for your peers always brings added pressures. *Grafik*'s readership had been predominantly student based, but SEA's brief was to redesign the magazine to appeal to a broader demographic. Its solution rationalized the existing design, retaining its energy within a functional and accessible structure. Developing a flexible grid was the key to this. The grid is multicolumn and also divides the page into a series of small horizontal fields. This structure supports various typographic devices—large indents and staggered text, along with continuous text, captions, standfirsts, and titling—and full-bleed, squared-up, and cut-out images.

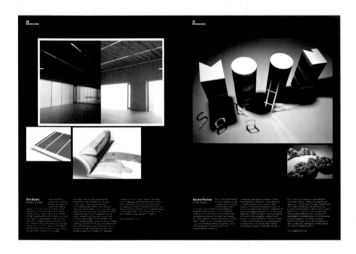

Grids: Creative Solutions for Graphic Designers

Joachim Schmid
The Photographers'
Gallery, London
Until 17 June
By Anghakd Lewis

Six Books

CAMOUFLAGE

FURNISH

100 years of Fashion Illustration

OPTIC NERVE

Mies van der Rohe

...ER CiTY

Insight

Always reaching for the same paper samples?
Then maybe it's time to try something new. We
asked the paper experts to give us the lowdown
on their hottest new products, and this is what
they came up with.

Xper by Fedrigoni

**Stucco Collection
by Fedrigoni**

**Zanders ZETA Bespoke
Watermark from M-real
Weights available**

**Stephen by Robert
Horne Weights available**

**Greencoat Matt Extra
by Howard Smith
Weights available**

**Take 2 Offset by
James McNaughton**

**Magnecote by
James McNaughton
Weights available?**

Trucard by Tullis Russell

Trucard ice

Trucard 2

PETER SAVILLE
FAC1-MCR

THURSDAY 30 NOVEMBER
6.30 LECTURE HALL

FAC1-MCR
Lecture poster designed by
AA Print Studio

THERE IS AN EXPECTAN[CY]
OF MANCHESTER

Peter Saville is a designer whose practice spans the fields of graphics, creative direction and art. Past clients have included Yohji Yamamoto, Christian Dior, Givenchy, and the Whitechapel Gallery.

I invited him to speak at the AA, a place that he hadn't visited for around 20 years, but he told me he hated preparing lectures. This isn't surprising. Saville's resumé is both extensive and complex, a testament to his creative restlessness and dogged desire for ultimate independence. So I struck a deal with him. I offered to put together an image-trawl through three decades of his work, the exact results of which he wasn't to find out until the conversation began that November evening.

My reasons to get Saville to talk at the AA were twofold. On the one hand, for a certain generation (often in their 30s and 40s) Saville's sumptuous visualisations were synonymous with the best of British pop culture: Joy Division, New Order, Factory Records to name a few. Beyond the nostalgia, though, Saville continues to inspire through his inimitable capacity to disown his status as a 'graphic designer' (a label he finds limiting) while being one of the most famous graphic designers living today. It's one of the reasons Manchester awarded him the job of 'art directing' its future cultural image.
Here are a few highlights from our conversation.

Shumon Basar, AACP Director

On being a graphic designer: 'I became a mercenary, a hired killer. I tried to work for clients who I didn't think were too bad. You have to work, to earn money and you just have to find a way to cope with that.'

On Joy Division's Unknown Pleasures: 'I hated the idea of things looking like record covers. If you put the name of the group on the front and put the title on the front it looks like a record cover. I did what I could with the elements – Joy Division gave me the wave pattern – but I didn't know anything, I had just left college…I wasn't even sure how you prepared artwork for print. I could only trust black and white….'

On New Order: 'The most enthusiastic reaction I got to any of the covers was "They don't much mind it." The worst was for Low-Life. When they saw it they all said, in unison, "You fucking bastard". Regret they liked because it was glossy and sexy … Bernard said, "We might fucking sell something with this one, Peter. How long has it taken?" But they never asked me about any of them, they weren't interested.'

On Yohji Yamamoto's 1991 menswear collection: 'He said, "I don't want to see the clothes. I don't want models." In other words, "I am sick of this … It doesn't make sense anymore." So I made a campaign that said as much. The company panicked, "This is financial suicide. We have to stop Peter, we have to stop Yohji, we have to stop it!".'

On Adidas limited edition Adicolor trainers: 'Adidas told me "Do what you want" but all of these brand partnerships are a lie… The brief made the truth plain to see, dictating the meaning of the word green. On page 1 they say I'm a "preeminent image-maker of my generation" and on page 5 they

Peter Saville logos
Various logos used in the early years of Saville's practice

Grids: Creative Solutions for Graphic Designers

GRID SPECIFICATIONS

Page size (trimmed)	176 x 250mm
Top margin	5mm
Bottom margin	24mm
Outside margin	10mm
Inside margin	20mm
Number of columns	4
Gutter width	5mm
Extras	Baseline grid, 12pt

AARCHITECTURE

Design: Wayne Daly and Grégory Ambos at AA Print Studio with Zak Group

AArchitecture is a "news-zine" published quarterly by the Architectural Association School of Architecture and designed by Wayne Daly and Grégory Ambos. The content is broad and designed to encourage debate. Sometimes spreads show a book-within-a-book, sometimes texts are indented and staggered, sometimes full-bleed color pages are used as part of the navigation. This playful layering of information reflects the purpose of the publication—to provide a discursive forum for students, tutors, and professionals to scrutinize and shape their subject. The four-column text grid appears to be only one of the publication's defining structures.

CRISTIANO TORALDO DI
SUPER...

---

mance goals, fosters innovation in construction.[6] Yet the role of architectural design within this context remains open to question. The latest update of the building regulations made performance evaluation more complex by introducing plant and equipment into the building's 'system performance'. This could potentially lead to environmental design principles being abandoned and the responsibility for 'making it work' being handed over to the building services engineer. Architecture could lose or give up its responsibility to perform if we no longer have environmental achievement 'per form' but only 'per system'.

An example of this scenario is apparent in the Thames Gateway, one of the UK's most celebrated 'sustainable' developments. Here architecture was used as a starting point, but the results disappointed the ambitious developer. The at times restrictive and limiting architectural features did not prove as effective at reducing carbon emissions as other on-site initiatives, such as those designed to reduce car usage. The developer has now changed approach, and in more recent projects has concentrated on embedded efficiency and low and zero carbon technologies (LZC), in physical as well as service infrastructures, to facilitate sustainable lifestyles.

Dialogue
The above examples demonstrate that many interpretations of environment and environmental performance are possible. The research cluster's ambition is to harness each group's engagement, knowledge and enthusiasm for research into EES design. In order not to be biased, the curators set out to develop a methodology that would identify research topics that address issues of interest to the design community but are also of scientific relevance. This ensures the interpretation of 'environment' matches the scale against which its performance is measured.

Cluster Activity
To gain an overview of current EES design activity the cluster organised an open competition. No specific subjects or categories were defined by the organising committee. The submissions document a self-assessment of our profession's ability to respond to environmental, ecological and sustainability-related challenges. Of particular interest are the definitions of 'environment' and 'environmental performance' of the individual entries.

The outcome of the competition and accompanying survey resulted in an exhibition preview hosted at the Architectural Association from 8 to 11 November 2006. The validity and importance of differing strands was examined during the event and recommendations

were made for future research activities. The winning and shortlisted entries were exhibited, and a book is forthcoming.

During the academic year the EES Research Cluster also facilitated open and informal roundtable discussions with participants from all realms of the built environment. The aim was to communicate the different stakeholders' views on performance-related issues to EES. Participants ranged from investors and developers, architects and engineers, planners and government officials to scientists, educators and students of all levels. The complexity of addressing multiple, often contradictory demands of performance was highlighted by the contrasting views.

Conclusion
The work of the EES Research Cluster has so far revealed that the terms 'environment' and 'performance' are used vaguely and are not defined rigorously enough to evaluate design performance. The survey information taken from the submissions to the Call for Projects awaits further investigation.

The intentions of the research cluster have been presented along with the methodology employed. Gathering and identifying these relevant research strands has been the main subject of the cluster's work to date, and it is hoped that this study will stimulate an ongoing discussion involving a wide audience that stretches beyond the educational setting and the architectural profession.

Acknowledgements
The authors would like to thank Brett Steele for his encouragement and the idea of creating the research clusters at the AA. The contributions of all discussion members, judges and participants are duly acknowledged.

This text is adapted from a paper published in 'PLEA Conference Proceedings 2006', the publication accompanying the 23rd Conference on Passive and Low Energy Architecture, Geneva, Switzerland, September 2006.

Werner Gaiser is a course tutor on the Sustainable Environmental Design MA programme and a Curator of the EES Research Cluster.
Steve Hardy is Unit Master of Diploma 16 and a Curator of the EES Research Cluster.

BOB MAXWELL'S LAST LECTURE

On Wednesday 22 November, an evening event was held to mark the decision of Bob Maxwell to give up his teaching on the Histories and Theories MA programme. He marked the occasion with a lecture entitled 'Maxwell's Last Lecture'. The lecture hall was packed with students, teachers and above all with several generations of professional colleagues and friends. He opened his lecture with a melancholy roll-call of all those who were absent by reason of death. Foremost in his mind was the figure of James Stirling. The evening was full of the memory of friends.

The lecture itself must have surprised some of his audience, who perhaps were expecting a more purely architectural topic. But the teacher in him was still passionately concerned with educating his fellow architects by introducing aspects of the human sciences which could illuminate architecture, and which could provide architects with an understanding of how all objects present meaning. Most of the lecture was devoted to an outline of subjects as it was understood by de Saussure and Roland Barthes. The concerns reflected on Bob's teaching, both while he had been Dean at Princeton University and in his teaching at the AA in the last two decades.

After the lecture tributes were paid to Bob by Ed Jones and Rick Mather, who spoke warmly of Bob as an architect and a friend. From his lecture the

audience were again made aware of the striking force of his complex character in which the twin aspects of Ulster Protestantism and Francophile Hedonism were intertwined. Above all the audience was aware of his underlying humanity, which has always shaped his students' experience of him.

By Mark Cousins, Director of Histories and Theories programme.

Bob Maxwell
Places were reserved long in advance for Bob Maxwell's last lecture

Grids: Creative Solutions for Graphic Designers

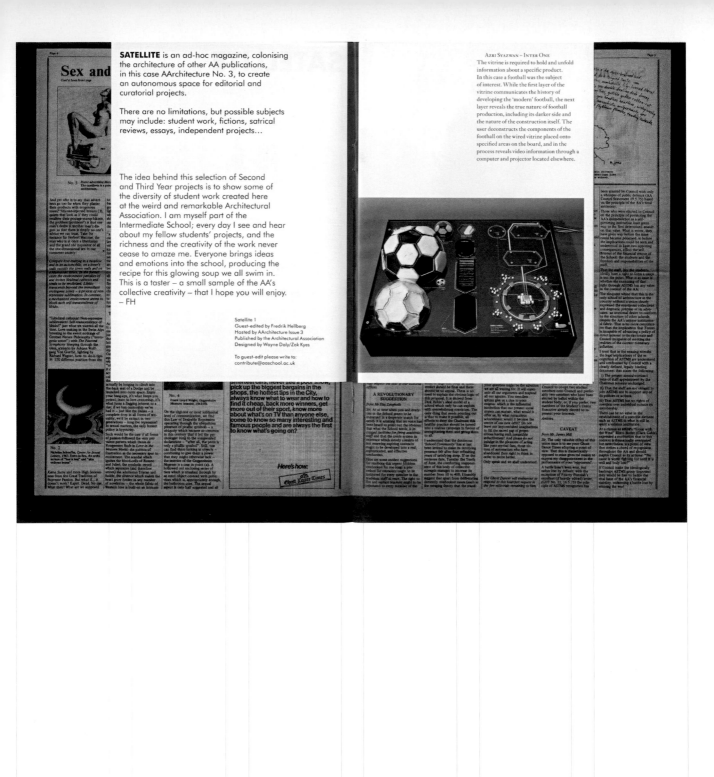

SATELLITE is an ad-hoc magazine, colonising the architecture of other AA publications, in this case AArchitecture No. 3, to create an autonomous space for editorial and curatorial projects.

There are no limitations, but possible subjects may include: student work, fictions, satrical reviews, essays, independent projects…

The idea behind this selection of Second and Third Year projects is to show some of the diversity of student work created here at the weird and remarkable Architectural Association. I am myself part of the Intermediate School; every day I see and hear about my fellow students' projects, and the richness and the creativity of the work never cease to amaze me. Everyone brings ideas and emotions into the school, producing the recipe for this glowing soup we all swim in. This is a taster – a small sample of the AA's collective creativity – that I hope you will enjoy.
– FH

Satellite 1
Guest-edited by Fredrik Hellberg
Hosted by AArchitecture Issue 3
Published by the Architectural Association
Designed by Wayne Daly/Zak Kyes

To guest-edit please write to:
contribute@aaschool.ac.uk

AZRI SYAZWAN – INTER ONE
The vitrine is required to hold and unfold information about a specific product. In this case a football was the subject of interest. While the first layer of the vitrine communicates the history of developing the 'modern' football, the next layer reveals the true nature of football production, including its darker side and the nature of the construction itself. The user deconstructs the components of the football on the wired vitrine placed onto specified areas on the board, and in the process reveals video information through a computer and projector located elsewhere.

AArchitecture
News from the Architectural Association

I DO NOT
WANT TO TALK TO
YOU ABOUT
ARCHITECTURE.
I DETEST
TALK ABOUT
ARCHITECTURE.

AArchitecture   Issue 4   Summer   2007   1

VERSO

AArchitecture
News from the Architectural Association
Issue 4 / Summer 2007
aaschool.net

©2007
All rights reserved.
Published by Architectural Association,
36 Bedford Square, London WC1B 3ES.

Contact:
contribute@aaschool.ac.uk
Nicola Quinn +44 (0) 207 887 4000

To send news briefs:
news@aaschool.ac.uk

EDITORIAL TEAM
Brett Steele, Editorial Director
Nicola Quinn, Managing Editor
Zak Kyes / Zak Group, Art Director
Wayne Daly, Graphic Designer
Alex Lorente
Fredrik Hellberg

ACKNOWLEDGEMENTS
Valerie Bennett
Pamela Johnston
Marilyn Sparrow
Hinda Sklar
Russell Bestley

Printed by Cassochrome, Belgium

CONTRIBUTORS

Rosa Ainley
<eventslist@aaschool.ac.uk>

Edward Bottoms
<edward@aaschool.ac.uk>

Mark Cousins
<markcousins@aaschool.ac.uk>

Wayne Daly
<daly_wa@aaschool.ac.uk>

Margaret Dewhurst
<margiedewhurst@hotmail.com>

Zak Kyes
<zz@zak.to>

Aram Mooradian
<aram.mooradian@gmail.com>

Harmony Murphy
<harmonymurphy@gmail.com>

Joel Newman
<joel@aaschool.ac.uk>

Kitty O'Grady
<ogrady_ki@aaschool.ac.uk>

Mark Prizeman

Simone Sagi
<simone@aaschool.ac.uk>

Vasilis Stroumpakos
<vasi@00110.org>

COVER

Front Cover:
Le Corbusier, AA after-dinner speech
1 April 1953

Front inner cover: Hans Scharoun's
Staatsbibliothek
Back inner cover: Peter Eisenman's
Memorial to the Murdered Jews of Europe
Photos: Timothy Deal, on AA Members'
trip to Berlin, 19–22 April 2007

* * * *

PEIGNOT

MARY TYLER MOORE
MARY TYLER MOORE

Headlines in the issue are set in Peignot,
a geometrically constructed sans-serif
display typeface designed by A. M.
Cassandre in 1937. It was commissioned
by the French foundry Peignot et Deberny.
The typeface is notable for not having
a traditional lower-case, but in its place
a 'multi-case' combining traditional
lower-case and small capital characters.
The typeface achieved some popularity
in poster and advertising publishing from
its release through the late 1940s. Use of
Peignot declined with the growth of the
International Typographic Style which
favoured less decorative, more objective
typeface. Peignot experienced a revival
in the 1970s as the typeface used on The
Mary Tyler Moore Show. While often
classified as 'decorative', the face is a
serious exploration of typographic form
and legibility.
Taken from:
http://en.wikipedia.org/wiki/Peignot

Body text is set in Sabon Bold.

Architectural Association (Inc.),
Registered Charity No. 311083. Company
limited by guarantee. Registered in
England No. 171402. Registered office
as above.

AArchitecture ISSUE 4 / SUMMER 2007

PATRICK BOUCHAIN:
KNOW-HOW/SAVOIR FAIRE PG 4
AA MEMBERS' VISIT: BERLIN PG 8
NORMAN KLEIN:
THE SPACE BETWEEN 1975–2050 PG 9
NEW MEDIA RESEARCH INITIATIVE PG 13
EVERYTHING YOU'VE EVER WANTED
TO KNOW ABOUT ORNAMENT PG 16
STREET FARMER PG 19
CORB AT THE AA PG 23
MARK COUSINS: THE UGLY PG 26
JOHN MACLEAN: BRASILIA PG 28
AA SUMMER PAVILION 2007 PG 30
DALE BENEDICT /
AA SECRETARY'S OFFICE PG 32
SOM AWARD / AA MEMBERS PG 33
AA NEWS BRIEFS PG 34

WE DO NOT KNOW EACH OTHER BUT WE READ EACH
OTHER AS SIGNS, WE BUILD UP A CODE OF
RECOGNITION THAT ENABLES US TO IDENTIFY PEOPLE
AND OBJECTS THROUGH THEIR ATTRIBUTES. MARK COUSINS PG 27

Grids: Creative Solutions for Graphic Designers

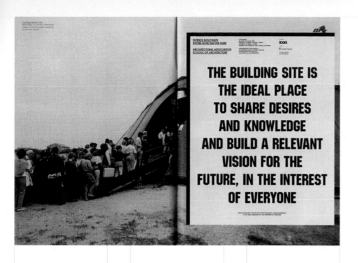

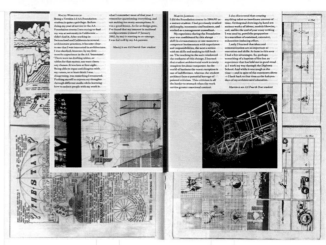

SIMON ESTERSON: You are one of the very few type designers to have worked with metal type-setting, then photosetting, through the digital revolution, and then on to screen-based, non-print media. How do you feel about what has happened to typeface design in the last 25 years?

MATTHEW CARTER: [laughs] It's been 50 years, by the way, since I left school and started working in type. I'm happy to have had a traditional training, although even by the late 1950s making type by hand was obsolete commercially speaking. It never really had a commercial application for me. It's been very interesting to live through these various changes in technology. Though most of type's history, sons, grandsons, great grandsons came and went and the technology never changed. The opposite has been true in the last 50 years: the technology has changed faster than the typefaces if anything. So it's been interesting.

My own feeling about it: if you took all of the things that go into making a typeface, and you gave them a score out of ten, I would say that the technical part of it is worth one or two on that scale. In other words, however the type is made, about at least 80 per cent of it is still the same, whatever tools you use. There are exceptions to that. When I worked on Bell Centennial for the United States phonebooks, where the environment it's used in is rather hostile, the technology played a larger part. For phone books, we're talking about six point type on newsprint. When I did the screen fonts for Microsoft, I think more than 20 percent of that was technical influence. So that's my feeling about it. A lot of people disagree and believe that type cut in steel has different qualities, and I can look at beautiful letterpress printing from metal type and I can see that things have been lost. But in my opinion the gains in digital type far outweigh the losses.

It's a fatuous thing to say in a way, but if I had my choice of period in which to have worked in this business I would choose exactly the one that I happen to have lucked into, precisely because of all these changes. I'm endlessly glad to have survived into the digital era because I regard that as the best technology we've ever had. There are some drawbacks, there have been some losses, but for me, it's just a dream.

Type designer Matthew Carter (facing page) was born in England in the 1930s. He trained as a punch cutter in the Netherlands before working as a typography consultant for Crosfield electronics. He later worked for Mergenthaler-Linotype in New York before becoming typography consultant to Her Majesty's Stationery Office in the 1980s. In 1981 he set up Bitstream Inc with Mike Parker in Massachusetts, the first independent American company to manufacture digital type. In 1992 he founded Carter & Cone Type Inc with Cherie Cone. Matthew Carter was named a Royal Designer for Industry in 1981. In his recent visit to London, Carter gave a talk at the Design Museum; for future events and exhibitions see www.designmuseum.org

Simon Esterson is a magazine and newspaper designer. He has been art director of The Guardian in London and creative director of Domus in Milan.

With thanks to the St Bride Printing Library

SE: I suppose designers who are used to working on a Mac, take being able to track and kern type for granted, when actually tracking and kerning with metal type-setting was very difficult, if not sometimes impossible.

MC: Kerning is a good example: strictly speaking, there was kerning in the latter days of film composition, there were some refinement programmes and so on, but essentially it became part of type with the coming of Type 1 PostScript fonts, True Type and so on. I regard kerning tables as a great blessing for typography.

SE: Once, the making of type was almost like a secret society: there was the mystique of being a punch-cutter and type-maker. Then it became quite an industrial process and Monotype and Linotype seemed to rule the world in composition terms: if they didn't make a typeface then it wasn't going to be made. Now, there's this incredible blossoming, where it seems as if everybody can be a type designer if they want to.

MC: I'm entirely happy about that. I'm sometimes a bit nostalgic about the time when it was a tiny club, when you had to go through painful initiations in order to be a type designer, but on balance, I'm glad the whole thing got blown wide open by the computer and particularly the coming of open font formats in the late 80s. There was a huge flow of interest in type design and it got democratised. There was no longer just a priesthood, but a sort of laity as well. I think a huge amount of very interesting work was done then, and some continues. What there is much more of, of course, are people who are primarily graphic designers or typographers, who occasionally make a typeface as a labour of love. This would have never happened in the old regime because it was just too hard to get started. Now, it's not uncommon to see student portfolios with typefaces they've designed and I'm completely delighted by that, it doesn't mean to say that everything made under those conditions are things that I like, but cream rises, and out of that ferment come very good things.

SE: Type design is quite stratified – even in the Victorian era you had display type and text type, and there's been a lot of activity in recent years in exuberant display typography. While you do some of these things too, a lot of your work is about what I'd call industrial-strength text typesetting.

MC: Yes, I think in my case there isn't a moral issue there, it's just a matter of temperament. Because I made my start in type founding, I never went to design school. I think that I've always been interested in these rather thorny, problem-solving projects, which are largely text faces. I have done a few display faces as well, but I seem to have mostly been asked to work in the text field, and I'm very happy with that. I don't think you're ever going to be a type designer unless you accept that you have to work within certain constraints.

SE: How does it work? Do you sit at home and wait for the phone to ring, with somebody saying 'we've got a problem,' or do you wake up in the morning thinking 'I have this beautiful idea for a lower case A, now I just need to do the rest of the alphabet?'

MC: I suppose both things happen. In an ideal world, life would be a nice balance between speculative projects and commissions. In fact I'm not good at bright ideas. If you sat me down in front of a blank computer screen on a Monday it would still be blank on the Friday. But if you said to me 'we have this typeface and it's a bit too heavy and too wide, fix it up,' I'd have something for you.

I tend not to get bolts from the blue very often although for example, a typeface like Mantinia was the direct result of going into an exhibition at the Royal Academy in 1992 and looking at some lettering there. I wish that happened more often, I wish I could say 'I'm going down that road now, I'm going to see a piece of vernacular lettering which is going to turn me on and become a wonderful typeface.' It doesn't normally happen.

SE: So it's not the case that you walk down the street and see so much inspiring typography...

MC: Obviously, I do see things I like, walking down the street, looking at books and so on. A good proportion of the faces that I've done have been based, to some degree, on historical models, and I'm interested in the history of typeface design, but, as you say, a lot of my faces do come about because somebody calls me up with a particular problem. ▶

A Life in Type

(Part One)

Matthew Carter is the world's leading type designer. In the apt setting of the St Bride Printing Library, editorial designer Simon Esterson talks to him about his 50 years in the industry. Continued next month

MANTINIA WAS THE DIRECT RESULT OF GOING INTO AN EXHIBITION AT THE ROYAL ACADEMY IN 1992 AND LOOKING AT SOME LETTERING THERE. I WISH THAT HAPPENED MORE OFTEN, I WISH I COULD SAY "I'M GOING DOWN THE ROAD NOW, I'M GOING TO SEE A PIECE OF VERNACULAR LETTERING WHICH IS GOING TO TURN ME ON AND BECOME A TYPEFACE."

Sports Illustrated asked me to design them a new text face, a bit heavier than Times, but no wider, because the editors didn't want to cut down on words, and I think they were absolutely right to say that – *why would they sacrifice their writing so that I can go to hell with myself and make some unsuitable typeface?*

To celebrate its seventieth anniversary, Penguin has commissioned the Pocket Penguins series: 70 covers from 70 different artists, who were paid just £70 each. By Steve Hare

For a graphic designer, having your own print works to play with must be just about the ultimate toy. Issay Kitagawa makes full use of his. By Patrick Burgoyne

GRID SPECIFICATIONS

Page size (trimmed)	280 x 280mm
Top margin	8mm
Bottom margin	18mm
Outside margin	8mm
Inside margin	18mm
Number of columns	15
Gutter width	4.5mm
Extras	N/A

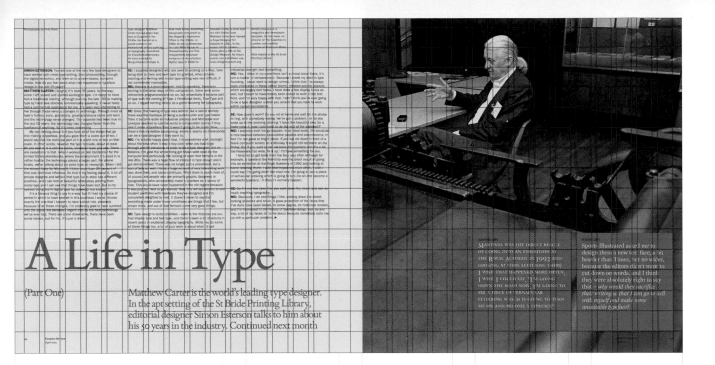

A Life in Type

(Part One)

Matthew Carter is the world's leading type designer. In the apt setting of the St Bride Printing Library, editorial designer Simon Esterson talks to him about his 50 years in the industry. Continued next month

CREATIVE REVIEW

Design: Nathan Gale at Creative Review

When the design magazine *Creative Review* was redesigned, it gave art director Nathan Gale an opportunity to introduce one grid that was flexible enough to accommodate all the different material the magazine shows. Previously it had used more than one grid, and Gale thought this was an opportune time to rationalize the design system. The new grid is multicolumn and divided into small horizontal fields. By combining columns and fields, text can run to the three different widths the magazine needs, and images of different sizes and scales can be positioned easily and flexibly.

ABRAM GAMES MAXIMUM MEANING FROM MINIMUM MEANS

By Carmen Martínez-López

Abram Games (1914-96) was one of the great poster designers of the 20th century. His contribution to the development of graphic communication was even more remarkable for having been made within the constricts of propaganda communication during World War II. Images such as *Your Talk May Kill Your Comrades* or *Don't Crow About What You Know About* applied modern design sophistication to the primary messages of wartime in a witty and effective way. Although Games' career coincided with the demise of his original trade as a graphic artist, as the promotional power of posters diminished in the face of television and colour supplements, he remained productive throughout. Following Games' death in 1996, the illustrator David Gentleman FCSD wrote that:

"All Abram Games' designs were recognisably his own. They had vigour, imagination, passion and individuality ... And he was lucky—and clever—in contriving, over a long and creative working life, to keep on doing what he did best."

SELECTED ILLUSTRATIONS
LEFT TO RIGHT

Festival of Britain, 1951
© Estate of Abram Games

British Railways poster
to promote tourism
in Blackpool, 1952
© Estate of Abram Games

London Underground, 1937
© Transport for London

CONCERTS

BALLET

OPERA

CHORAL

RECITALS

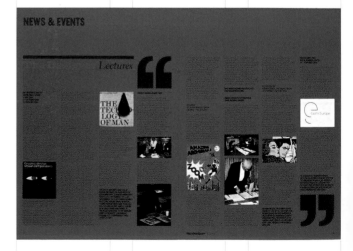

NEWS & EVENTS

Lectures

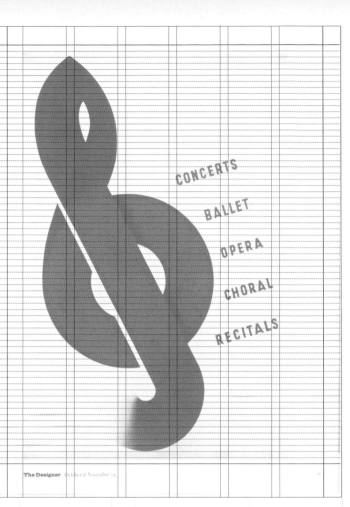

ABRAM GAMES MAXIMUM MEANING FROM MINIMUM MEANS

By Carmen Martinez-López

Abram Games (1914-96) was one of the great poster designers of the 20th century. His contribution to the development of graphic communication was even more remarkable for having been made within the constricts of propaganda communication during World War II. Images such as *Your Talk May Kill Your Comrades* or *Don't Grow About What You Know About* applied modern design sophistication to the primary messages of wartime in a witty and effective way. Although Games' career coincided with the demise of his original trade as a graphic artist, as the promotional power of posters diminished in the face of television and colour supplements, he remained productive throughout. Following Games' death in 1996, the illustrator David Gentleman FCSD wrote that:

"All Abram Games' designs were recognisably his own. They had vigour, imagination, passion and individuality ... And he was lucky—and clever—in contriving, over a long and creative working life, to keep on doing what he did best."

SELECTED ILLUSTRATIONS
LEFT TO RIGHT

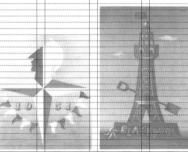

CONCERTS
BALLET
OPERA
CHORAL
RECITALS

The Designer October & November

GRID SPECIFICATIONS

Page size (trimmed)	297 x 210mm
Top margin	12mm
Bottom margin	21.1mm
Outside margin	10mm
Inside margin	10mm
Number of columns	6
Gutter width	5mm
Extras	Baseline grid, 11pt starting at 12mm

THE DESIGNER

Design: Brad Yendle at Design Typography

The Designer is a 32-page magazine produced every month by the Chartered Society of Designers. Given its readership, any redesign would be a tough brief, particularly as the objective was to increase appeal by injecting visual excitement. Inspired by the work of Willy Fleckhaus and Simon Esterson, designer Brad Yendle introduced a simple six-column grid. By combining columns, this could accommodate text and a variety of picture sizes. Yendle paid particular attention to typographic detailing, making sure that the choice of font, type sizes, and leading gave optimum legibility in his three-column text structure.

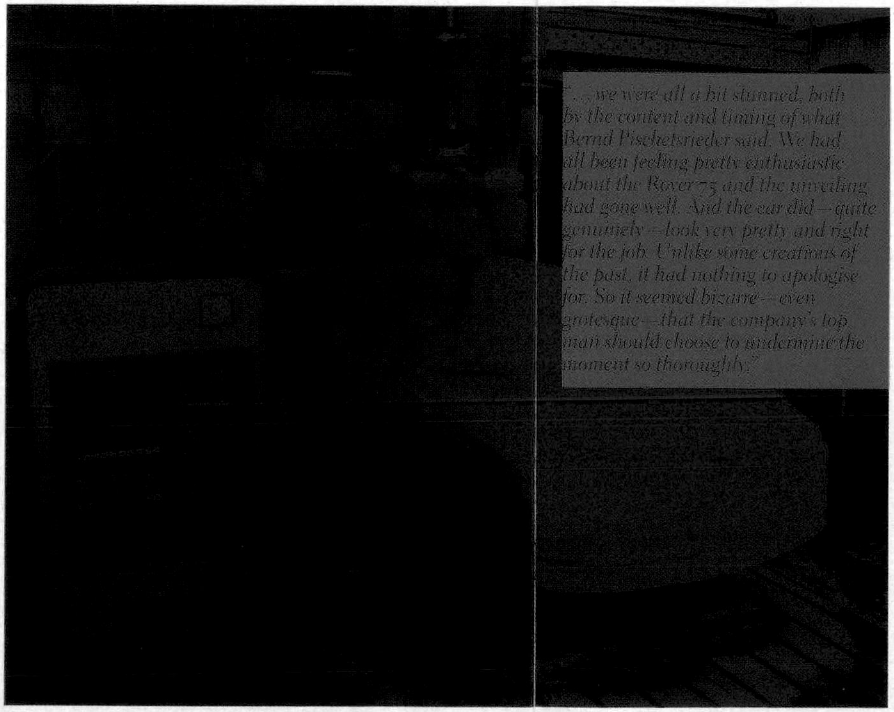

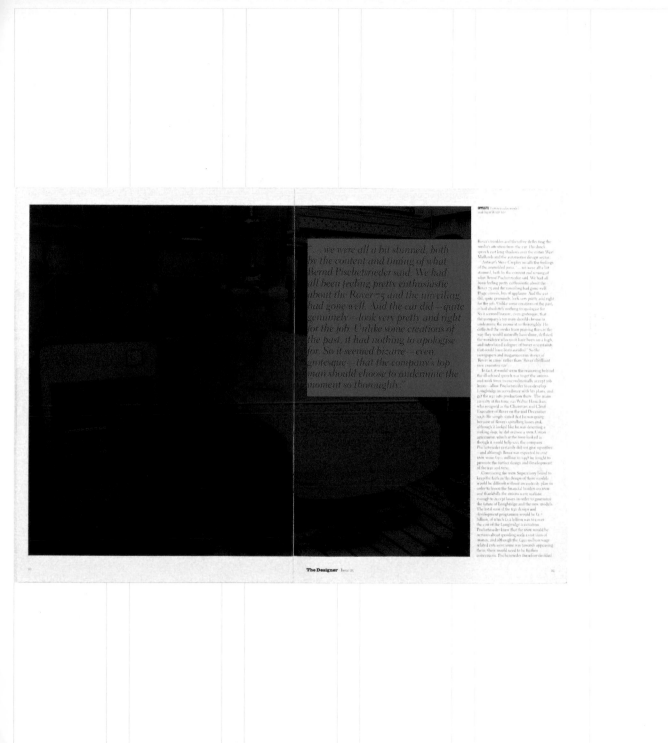

"...we were all a bit stunned, both by the content and timing of what Bernd Pischetsrieder said. We had all been feeling pretty enthusiastic about the Rover 75 and the unveiling had gone well. And the car did—quite genuinely—look very pretty and right for the job. Unlike some creations of the past, it had nothing to apologise for. So it seemed bizarre—even grotesque—that the company's top man should choose to undermine the moment so thoroughly."

Rover's troubles and therefore deflecting the media's attention from the car. His shock speech cast long shadows over the entire West Midlands and the automotive design sector.

Autocar's Steve Cropley recalls the feelings of the assembled press: '...we were all a bit stunned, both by the content and timing of what Bernd Pischetsrieder said. We had all been feeling pretty enthusiastic about the Rover 75 and the unveiling had gone well. Huge crowds, lots of applause. And the car did, quite genuinely, look very pretty and right for the job. Unlike some creations of the past, it had absolutely nothing to apologise for. So it seemed bizarre, even grotesque, that the company's top man should choose to undermine the moment so thoroughly. He deflected the media from praising the car the way they would naturally have done, deflated the workforce who must have been on a high, and introduced a degree of buyer uncertainty that could have been avoided.' So the newspapers and magazines ran stories of 'Rover in crisis' rather than 'Rover's brilliant new executive car'.

In fact, it would seem the reasoning behind the ill-advised speech was to get the unions and work force to unconditionally accept job losses – allow Pischetsrieder to redevelop Longbridge in accordance with his plans, and get the R30 into production there. The main casualty at the time was Walter Hasselkus, who resigned as the Chairman and Chief Executive of Rover on the 2nd December 1998. He simply stated that he was going because of Rover's spiralling losses and, although it looked like he was deserting a sinking ship, he did oversee a BMW/Union agreement, which at the time looked as though it would help save the company. Pischetsrieder certainly did not give up either – and although Rover was expected to cost BMW some £400 million in 1998 he fought to promote the further design and development of the R30 and MINI.

Convincing the BMW Supervisory board to keep the faith in the design of these models would be difficult without an austerity plan in order to lessen the financial burden on BMW and thankfully the unions were realistic enough to accept losses in order to guarantee the future of Longbridge and the new models. The total sum of the R30 design and development programme would be £1.7 billion, of which £1.2 billion was to cover the cost of the Longbridge renovation. Pischetsrieder knew that the BMW would be nervous about spending such a vast sum of money, and although the £450 million wage related cuts went some way towards appeasing them, there would need to be further concessions. Pischetsrieder therefore decided

The Designer Issue 25

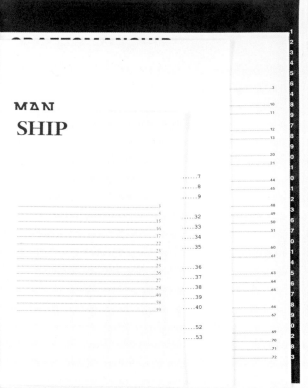

MAN

SHIP

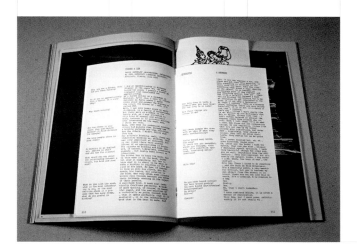

The Letter Home

GRID SPECIFICATIONS

Page size (trimmed)	210 x 297mm
Format/Grid 1	200 x 270mm
Format/Grid 2	185 x 239mm
Format/Grid 3	146 x 234mm
Format/Grid 4	115 x 185mm
Number of columns	N/A
Gutter width	N/A
Extras	N/A

GRAY MAGAZINE
Design: Clare McNally, Lane Gry, and Risto Kalmre

GRAy is the official magazine of the Gerrit Rietveld Academy in Amsterdam. An annual publication, it is designed, edited, and produced by graduating graphic design students. The three designers, Clare McNally, Lane Gry, and Risto Kalmre, wanted *GRAy* to reflect its theme—craftsmanship—partly through its precision, but also through their hands-on skill in putting it together. They evolved two approaches to the grid.

The first grid was derived from the different formats of various types of publication: the novel, the art book, technical manuals, and A4 (210 x 297mm [c. 8⅛ x 11⅝in]) magazines. These four formats were amalgamated to form the underlying structure governing the placement text and images.

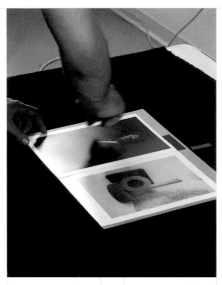

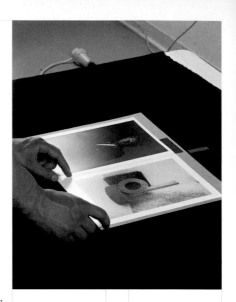

A test scan using the reprographic scanner.

Each spread was laid out by hand as an "image."

The day of scanning.

The scan of pages 2 and 3.

The second grid was generated in InDesign to give a consistent position for folios and running feet. Each section of the magazine was printed and cut out according to the various formats. These spreads were then positioned by hand according to the InDesign grid, then scanned and reprinted, making the final design process interactive in a totally physical way.

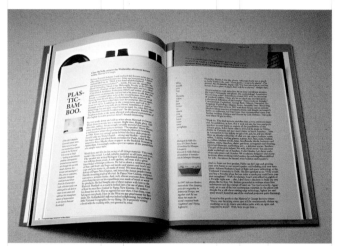

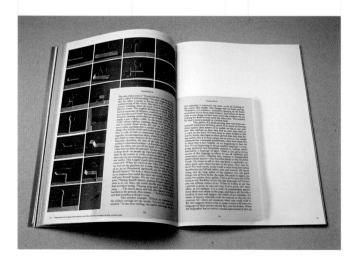

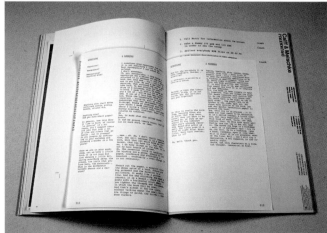

DUMB PLANETS ARE ROUND TOO

Artist_John Isaacs

Last night I dreamt that I lived in the ocean. I felt safe with all these fish swimming around me, it never occurred to me that they would eat me. I felt that because I was not hungry that they too were not thinking about food. Even the sharks, which would normally scare me to death, seemed to pay me no interest.

Of course I wasn't really there, so it's possible that I was invisible to all these creatures. Though it was strange to be underwater, it didn't feel unnatural. I had no trouble holding my breath, and I felt incredibly relaxed watching them all move so silently and effortlessly through the water. The way we

were down there me and the fish - was very laid back.

Then it occurred to me that people don't really like one another. That they do all these terrible things to one another for reasons they themselves cannot begin to explain, and even when they love one another and truly believe this to be the case there's always something in the way. I started to understand that people are all essentially alone. Outcasts not just from nature, but one another.

In the ocean everything is what it is.

The oddest looking creature is that way for

a reason, a function, but for us it is different. With all that we have, we are beyond evolution, beyond time to the extent that each person represents their own cosmos - a species evolving from birth to extinction at death. It is consciousness, which brings us apart.

This realisation started to merge into others, I lost track, got confused, and possibly a little anxious, trying both to follow and remember my thoughts. It was as though I was witnessing an immense explosion, which contained all the components of it's origin within the fragmentary pieces flying through space. People I never knew drifted next to more

familiar faces. Everyone that ever lived, and that ever would, everything ever made and that would be invented, spread out from the center of this thought and at just the point when I was beginning to loose sight of the edges it stopped still and took on the appearance of a huge cloud. I then felt rather than saw, that everyone was connected to one another by thin nerve like threads, which became visible as I thought about them. It was impossible to tell which one came before the other or if my thought and their appearance were simultaneous. Everything was there.

I saw you in there too.

Façade

Artist_Name Here

DUMB PLANETS ARE ROUND TOO

Artist: John Isaacs

Last night I dreamt that I lived in the ocean. I felt safe with all these fish swimming around me, it never occurred to me that they would eat me. I felt that because I was not hungry that they too were not thinking about food. Even the sharks, which would normally scare me to death, seemed to pay me no interest.

Of course I wasn't really there, so it's possible that I was invisible to all these creatures. Though it was strange to be underwater, it didn't feel unnatural, I had no trouble holding my breath, and I felt incredibly relaxed watching them all move so silently and effortlessly through the water. The way we

were down there me and the fish - was very laid back.

Then it occurred to me that people don't really like one another. That they do all these terrible things to one another for reasons they themselves cannot begin to explain, and even when they love one another and truly believe this to be the case there's always something in the way. I started to understand that people are all essentially alone. Outcasts not just from nature, but one another.

In the ocean everything is what it is.

The oddest looking creature is that way for

a reason, a function, but for us it is different. With all that we have, we are beyond evolution, beyond time to the extent that each person represents their own cosmos - a species evolving from birth to extinction at death. It is consciousness, which brings us apart.

This realisation started to merge into others, I lost track, got confused, and possibly a little anxious, trying both to follow and remember my thoughts. It was as though I was witnessing an immense explosion, which contained all the components of it's origin within the fragmentary pieces flying through space. People I never knew drifted next to more

familiar faces. Everyone that ever lived, and that ever would, everything ever made and that would be invented, spread out from the center of this thought and at just the point when I was beginning to loose sight of the edges it stopped still and took on the appearance of a huge cloud. I then felt rather than saw, that everyone was connected to one another by thin nerve like threads, which became visible as I thought about them. It was impossible to tell which one came before the other or if my thought and their appearance were simultaneous. Everything was there.

GRID SPECIFICATIONS

Page size (trimmed)	235 x 304mm
Top margin	7mm
Bottom margin	20mm
Outside margin	7mm
Inside margin	15mm
Number of columns	5
Gutter width	7mm
Extras	Baseline grid, 6mm

NEXT LEVEL: STORYTELLERS

Design: Julian Harriman-Dickinson at Harriman Steel

Each issue of *Next Level*, a biannual photography, arts, and ideas magazine, is based on a different theme, and the design reflects this. From font usage to grid systems, each issue is designed from scratch. The theme of this issue was film. The color palette is derived from TV color bands and designer Julian Harriman-Dickinson introduced test cards as novel graphic devices. He wanted his design to be "so clear and transparent that my mum could see how it was done," so he deliberately foregrounded the five-column grid.

On Par

PHotoEspaña, now in its 8th year, took place
from 1st June to the 17th July across 50 galleries
in Madrid and showed the work of nearly 100
international photographers. It was a group portrait
of La Cuidad/The City, exploring the parameters of
21st Century city living and a variety of issues were
brought to the fore: What are the visions of utopia
and dystopia? What are the changing relationships
between public and private spheres, the centre and
the periphery? What are the consequences of post
industrial economies on the urban fabric? How have
urban policies altered the experience of the city?
What are the domestic preoccupations of the way
we live today?

TAKE CARE OF YOUR SCARF TATJANA

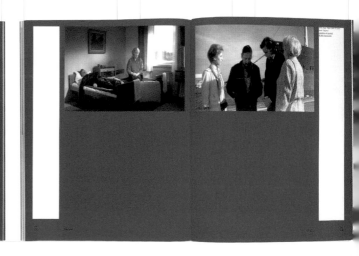

Special Guest Chris Marker /
Retrospective for the Paris daily
Libération. /
Originally published in Libération,
March 5, 2003, translated by /
Antoine de Baecque.

Q: Do you prefer television, movies on a big screen, or surfing the Internet?

I have a completely schizophrenic relationship with television. When I'm feeling lonely, I adore it, particularly since there's been cable. It's curious how cable offers an entire catalog of antidotes to the poisons of standard TV. If one network shows a ridiculous TV movie about Napoleon, you can flip over to the History Channel to hear Henri Guillemin's brilliantly mean commentary on it. If a literary program makes us submit to a parade of currently fashionable female monsters, we can change over to Mezzo to contemplate the luminous face of Hélène Grimaud surrounded by her wolves, and it's as if the others never existed. Now there are moments when I remember I am not alone, and that's when I fall apart. The exponential growth of stupidity and vulgarity is something that everyone has noticed, but it's not just a vague sense of disgust - it's a concrete quantifiable fact (you can measure it by the volume of the cheers that greet the talk-show hosts, which have grown by an alarming number of decibels in the last five years) and a crime against humanity. Not to mention the permanent aggressions against the French language. . . . And since you are exploiting my Russian penchant for confession, I must say the worst: I am allergic to commercials. In the early Sixties, making commercials was perfectly acceptable; now, it's something that no one will own up to. I can do nothing about it. This manner of placing the mechanism of the lie in the service of praise has always irritated me, even if I have to admit that this diabolical patron has occasionally given us some of the most beautiful images you can see on the small screen (have you seen the David Lynch commercial with the blue lips?). But cynics always betray themselves, and there is a small consolation in the industry's own terminology: they stop short of calling themselves so they call themselves creatives.

And the movies in all this?

For the reasons mentioned above, and under the orders of Jean-Luc, I've said for a long time that films should be seen first in theaters, and that television and video are only there to refresh your memory. Now that I no longer have any time at all to go to the cinema, I've started seeing films by lowering my eyes, with an ever increasing sense of sinfulness (this interview is indeed becoming Dostoevskian). But to tell the truth I no longer watch many films, only those by friends, or curiosities that an American acquaintance tapes for me on TCM. There is too much to see on the news, on the music channels or on the indispensable Animal Channel. And I feed my hunger for fiction with what is by far the most accomplished source: those great American TV series, like The Practice. There is a knowledge in them, a sense of story and economy, of ellipsis, a science of framing and of cutting, a dramaturgy and an acting style that has no equal anywhere, and certainly not in Hollywood.

Q: La Jetée inspired a video by David Bowie and a film by Terry Gilliam. And there's also a bar called 'La Jetée' in Japan. How do you feel about this cult? Does Terry Gilliam's imagination intersect with yours?

Terry's imagination is rich enough that there's no need to play with comparisons. Certainly, for me 12 Monkeys is a magnificent film (there are people who think they are flattering me by saying otherwise, that La Jetée is much better - the world is a strange place). It's just one of the happy signs, like Bowie's video, like the bar in Shinjuku (Hello, Tomoyo! To know that for almost 40 years, a group of Japanese are getting slightly drunk beneath my images every night - that's worth more to me than any number of Oscars!), that have accompanied the strange destiny of this particular film. It was made like a piece of automatic writing. I was filming Le Joli mai, completely immersed in the reality of Paris 1962, and the euphoric discovery of direct cinema (you will never make me say 'cinema verité') and on the crew's day off, I photographed a story I didn't completely understand. It was in the editing that the pieces of the puzzle came together, and it wasn't me who designed the puzzle. I'd have a hard time taking credit for it. It just happened, that's all.

Q: You are a witness of history. Are you still interested in world affairs? What makes you jump to your feet, react, shout?

Right now there are some very obvious reasons to jump, and we know them all so well that I have very little desire to talk more about them. What remains are the small, personal resentments. For me, 2002 will be the year of a failure that will never pass. It begins with a flashback, as in The Barefoot Contessa. Among our circle in the Forties, the one we all considered to be a future great writer was François Vernet. He had already published three books, and the fourth was to be a collection of short stories that he had written during the Occupation, with a vigor and an insolence that obviously left him little hope with the censors. The book wasn't published until 1945. Meanwhile, François had died in Dachau. I don't mean to label him as a martyr - that's not my style. Even if this death puts a kind of symbolic seal on a destiny that was already quite singular, the texts themselves are of such a rare quality that there is no need for reasons other than literary in order to love them and introduce them to others. François Maspero wasn't wrong when he said in an article that they "transverse time with only an extreme lightness of being as ballast." Because last year a courageous publisher, Michel Reynaud (Tirésias), fell in love with the book and took the risk of reprinting it.

I did everything I could to mobilize people I knew, not in order to make it the event of the season but simply to get it talked about. But no, there were too many books during that season. Except for Maspero, there wasn't a word in the press. And so - failure.

Q: Was that reaction too personal?

By chance, it was paired with a similar event, to which no line of friendship attached me. The same year, Capriccio Records released a new recording by Viktor Ullman. Under his name alone, this time. Previously, he and Gideon Klein had been recorded as Theresienstadt composers (for younger readers: Theresienstadt was the model concentration camp designed to be visited by the Red Cross, the Nazis made a film about it called The Führer Gives a City to the Jews.) With the best intentions in the world, [calling them] that was a way of putting them both back in the camp. If Messiaen had died after he composed the 'Quartet for the End of Time', would he be the prison camp composer?

This record is astounding: it contains lieder based on texts by Hölderlin and Rilke, and one is struck by the vertiginous thought that, at that particular time, no one was glorifying the true German culture more than this Jewish musician who was soon to die at Auschwitz. This time, there wasn't total silence - just a few flattering lines on the arts pages. Wasn't it worth a bit more? What makes me mad isn't that what we call "media coverage" is generally reserved for people I personally find rather mediocre - that's a matter of opinion and I wish them no ill. It's that the noise, in the electronic sense, just gets louder and louder and ends up drowning out everything, until it becomes a monopoly just like the way supermarkets force out the corner stores. That the unknown writer and the brilliant musician have the right to the same consideration as the corner store keeper may be too much to ask. And as long as you've handed me the microphone, I would add one more name to my list of the little injustices of the year: no one has said enough of the most beautiful book I have read for a long time, short stories again - La Fiancée d'Odessa, by [filmmaker] Edgardo Cozarinsky.

Q: Have your travels made you suspicious of dogmatism?

I think I was already suspicious when I was born. I must have traveled a lot before then!

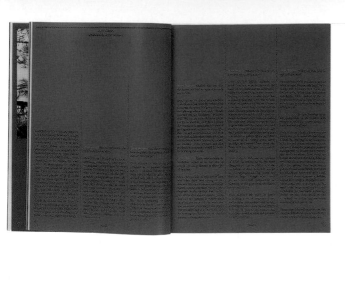

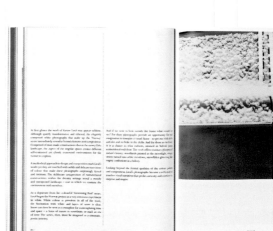

Grids: Creative Solutions for Graphic Designers

GRID SPECIFICATIONS

Page size (trimmed)	235 x 304mm
Top margin	9mm
Bottom margin	30mm
Outside margin	9mm
Inside margin	15mm
Number of columns	5
Gutter width	7mm
Extras	N/A

NEXT LEVEL: IF...

Design: Nick Steel at Harriman Steel

Next Level, a themed photography, arts, and ideas magazine, is produced twice a year. Each theme calls for a different design. This issue was inspired by the idea of simplification. Designer Nick Steel wanted the publication to be visually naive. He introduced larger-than-standard type for the body copy, and alternates between very simple two- and three-column grids. Space is introduced where possible, and images are generally squared up as determined by the grid.

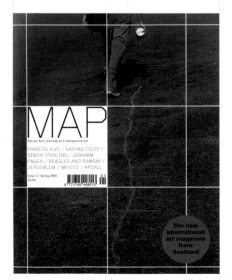

Grids: Creative Solutions for Graphic Designers

Moira Jeffrey *travels to Monterrey and discovers bright lights at* Sodium and Asphalt, *a major showing of 12 British artists in Mexico*

GRID SPECIFICATIONS

Page size (trimmed)	221 x 277mm
Top margin	10mm
Bottom margin	20mm
Outside margin	10mm
Inside margin	18mm
Number of columns	12
Gutter width	3mm
Extras	Baseline grid, 10.5pt

MAP MAGAZINE

Design: Matt Willey and Zoë Bather

MAP is an international art magazine published in Scotland. From the outset, designers Matt Willey and Zoë Bather felt a duty to display the work in a visually arresting, yet respectful and clear way. Willey and Bather took the rich, but functional language of cartography as their visual starting point. The grid on the cover divides the space so that the masthead can occupy any of six possible positions, depending upon its relationship to the image behind. The same grid determines the position of the standfirsts that announce each article. The grid on the review pages is plotted using cross-marks that borrow from the language of maps, while the navigation system uses blue vertical lines positioned next to the folios like lines of longitude.

Still, all is well, because we are each given the beautifully designed catalogue of Morrison's most recent show, and the paintings of slate quarries and cottages in the Easdale area, with the sea and islands looming, do make a positive impact. Apparently, Jolomo has had a couple of exhibitions organised by Kranenburg and Fowler on the Caledonian MacBrayne ferry. But there is no such luck for us, and our boat to Mull does not even have 'WE ARE NOT AFRAID OF THE INNER HEBRIDES' emblazoned along its flank. Nevertheless, we travel across the water in good spirits, with one wearing a brand new Oban-bought t-shirt that sports the slogan 'BOOTY FUN CLUB'. We give Mull a good going over. At least we

AND MULL

Focus
São Paolo Bienal..............50

Glasgow
Torsten Lauschmann..........52
Michael Fullerton............52
Kate Davis...................53

Paris
Thomas Hirschhorn..........54

Stirling
Rings of Saturn..............55

Washington DC
Dan Flavin...................56

Edinburgh
Mat Collishaw...............57
Andy Warhol................57
Ellen Gallagher.............58
Holbein to Hockney........59

Aberdeen
Urban Atlas................59

London
Camilla Løw................60
Faces in the Crowd........61

'Once there was a man who … washed a block of ice across a vast city until it melted and disappeared; an artist who sent a peacock to take his place in an important gathering of his peers; a man who persuaded a small army of workers to move an immense sand dune armed only with shovels; a solitary walker who one day emerged from a shop holding a loaded pistol …'

STUDIO

Grids: Creative Solutions for Graphic Designers

grotesque visions of railway architecture, a mish-mash of Otto Wagner urbanity and Bruno Gothick fantasy, complete with verbose quotes from an unknown source. Whether capricious or designed, both this and 'Mama, I got burned', on the opposite wall, are funny in a *Big Night Out* kind of way – a marriage of the avant-garde and kitsch.

At the back of the first room, Piper's *Double Door* divides the usually open-plan (or at least open *deep*) gallery into two separate spaces by means of swinging saloon doors. The centre of the doors is pierced by a cut-out star shape, which serves to frame the fixed, smiling face of the endlessly hula-hooping woman in 'Loop', Maurice Doherty's double-sided video projection in the room beyond. The doors, unmistakably celluloid-inspired, are such that the temptation to burst, rather than walk through, is hard to resist, and gallery etiquette is put at risk by the potential actions of wannabe cowboys.

This feast of Saturnalia may not be as licentious as its Roman precedent, but it's similarly impious, peppered with visual mockery and, like W.G Sebald's book which shares its title, the *Rings of Saturn* might well be a meditation on the possibly restorative powers of art.

Susannah Thompson is an art writer and lecturer at Glasgow School of Art.

Changing Room Gallery
3 Nov – 18 Dec 2004

Dan Flavin
Washington DC

Dan Flavin's was once reputed a difficult art – a fact difficult to grasp retrospectively when it can be seen for its sheer beauty. Should we now try to recapture the old sense of obduracy and negation, or rather give ourselves over to the visual fascination exercised by Flavin's bundles of light? Walking through the National Gallery, where Flavin's retrospective premiered before moving on to Fort Worth, then an international tour set to continue through 2007, it's easy to decide on the second course. The installation is ravishing, and the artist's ever-increasing mastery of his chosen medium, white and coloured fluorescent light in real architectural space, becomes patent as one follows his progress: from the early 'icons' (Johnson painted monochrome boxes mounted with fluorescent or, more often, incandescent bulbs) through the inaugural pure fluorescent piece, 'the diagonal of May 25, 1963 (to Constantin Brancusi)' – a eureka point in Flavin's story comparable to, say, 'Onement I' (1948), in Barnett Newman's marking the moment of greatest conceivable reduction or contraction (the Kabalistic *zimzum* that gave its name to one of Newman's sculptures) in which it momentarily seemed that 'little artistic craft (could be possible but from which all further creation would proceed. And then the polychromatic mixes with which Flavin began experimenting in 1964 but which really took off in richness and complexity around 1970, when Flavin made 'untitled

(to Barnett Newman) to commemorate his simple problem, red, yellow, and blue?' As shown by this corner construction with its vertical red and blue lights facing away from the open space and back toward the wall while the horizontal yellow fluorescent tubes face outward, the 'simple' combination of three primary colours as they interfuse in space becomes something almost ungraspable, and indeed escapes language altogether with resulting colour combinations no longer nameable red, yellow, or blue.

What this indicates is that although reality remains secreted within the suave beauty of Flavin's 'propositions' – an intellectual rather than an emotional difficulty, at least for the viewer. All the more curious, then, that it should have taken such an irascible character to produce this work. Although Flavin famously wrote of his material as 'common light repeated effulgently across anybody's wall' and of his subject as 'a neutral pleasure of seeing known to everyone', he was in fact notably possessive, one might even say illiberally close-fisted about the notion of his art, compulsively but always eloquently 'deflecting away from the methodological comprehension of his work', as Jack Burnham put it. Whereas most artists seem to believe that their work will unfold itself through time to reveal unforeseeable meaning, Flavin mused of leaving 'a will and testament to declare everything void at my death … because only I know this work as it ought to be. All posthumous interpretations are less.' Robert Morris, of course, had already made 'Statement of Aesthetic Withdrawal' (1963) removing 'all esthetic quality and content' from a previous work of his but the result was the addition of a new work, not the subtraction of an existing one from what Arthur C. Danto would dub 'the art world' – meaning, not the social milieu of artists, dealers, collectors, and so on, but the realm of things, accepted at a given point in history as belonging to art. No more could Flavin have asserted the ultimate control over the artistic existence of his work by the supreme and sovereign act of disowning it, yet he needed to believe in such control in order to produce something true enough to escape it. His art's posthumous existence cannot be switched off like an electric light; despite all the situational uncertainties that surround the effort to represent the effects he sought, the work continues to shine forth, expansively.

Barry Schwabsky is an art critic and author of The Widening Circle: Consequences of Modernism in Contemporary Art (Cambridge University Press) and Opera: Poems 1981–2002 (San Francisco: Meritage Press)

National Gallery of Art Washington DC
3 Oct 2004 – 9 Jan 2005

Left: 'The diagonal of May 25, 1963 (to Constantin Brancusi)'
Dan Flavin 1963

Mat Collishaw
Edinburgh

Mat Collishaw flatters to deceive. His best known work takes the form of exquisite photographs of flowers whose petals, on closer inspection, have been electronically replaced by close-ups of human skin diseases. Alongside these are his video installations: in one example, a video projection onto an ornate free-standing vanity mirror, depicting a beautiful young girl brushing her long blonde locks, fades into an image of what might well be the same girl 75 years later, still brushing, brushing, brushing her hair. Elsewhere, it's the deceptive power of the medium itself that interests Collishaw; an image of prisoners at the Abu Ghraib prison camp in Iraq is rendered in the form of a room-sized mosaic – in which a highly pixelated internet image provides the pattern for a craft form that originated in Persia, and provided the spoils of war in a different age.

Collishaw's largest solo exhibition to date is located in the beautifully restored Inverleith House, and it comes at an important time for an artist who – amazingly – emerged from the epicentre of Young British Art without having been ripped apart by the media. How could Tracey Emin's (now ex) long-term lover have avoided the same tabloid mauling that was the daily grind for Tracey, Damien, Sarah and Gillian for so much of the past decade? Maybe it is precisely because this work is so hard to pin down. It can be so wilfully artificial that it feels resistant, even at times slippery.

Looking at a projection of blurry photos of victims of Operation Barbarossa lying dead in the frozen Russian winter, you steel yourself for some grim thoughts about the atrocities of the German-Russian war in the early 1940s. But no sooner have you prepped yourself for this emotional onslaught,

than the image literally fizzles and melts away, as if the transparency inside the slide projector has just been destroyed by the heat. Again and again a grainy fuzzy image bubbles into oblivion, just as its content is becoming clear. It is hard to trust your judgement in Collishaw's work, because there's always a sense that, once you succumb to the sheer power or beauty of what you first see, that emotional response will be undermined by the realisation that things are definitely not what they first seemed.

In the end Collishaw's work frustrates because, despite its often very powerful ideas, it doesn't allow the viewer enough room in the work to engage with the artist's vision. Certainly, there's a sense that Collishaw's interests are sharply political. Yet by dickering about with the medium, he undermines the complexity of his message. Again and again he reminds us that what we see may not actually be the whole truth – but in the process each time he gives the impression that, when we get anywhere near his heartfelt convictions, he doesn't in fact hold them at all.

Staring at the 'Infectious Orchid' photographs with their skin-diseased petals, I found myself trying to think of something other than the trite aphorism, 'beauty is only skin deep', and wishing I could get to an understanding of his passions that went a little deeper.

Nick Barley is editor of The List.

Inverleith House
15 Jan – 13 Mar 2005

Andy Warhol:
Self Portraits
Edinburgh

'He was always such a strong, strong man/ I saw him go to pieces/ I saw him go to pieces'

'Pieces of a Man' – Gil Scott-Heron's 1971 hymn to his disenfranchised father could well have been penned after wandering the rooms housing this remarkably complete collection of Warhol's self portraits. Following a trajectory of gauche vulgarity, enthusiasm and playfulness through a tunnel of darkness into vanity and morbidity, his portraits move to a final reduction of form that, like the man himself in his later years, is almost translucent. At his best and worst Warhol was gifted and truly godless in his experimentation and this superb exhibition runs the gamut of the pope of pop art's (self) reflections and creativity.

Opening with Warhol's early childish but oddly effective graphite on paper sketches, his influence on future artists, even as a boy, can be identified in a drawing of Clint Hamilton, Nathan Gluck and himself (nicely stained with what looks like coffee). This graphite and coloured pencil sketch on Strathmore paper can now be seen as the reference point for a composition to which fellow artists David Hockney and Dennis Hopper (as photographer) frequently returned.

What follows next serves to illustrate what a funny, silly and joyful artist Warhol could be. His youthful visage bursts out of blue, pink and yellow acrylic screen prints; in some he looks like the Jackal, in others like blonde

Above left: 'Burning Flower'
Collishaw, 2004
Left: Early Self-Portrait
Andy Warhol, 1964

GRI

Pag

Top

Bott

Out...

Insi

Num

Gutt

Extr

Certain of NOTHING:

150_151

PREMIUM DENIM

86 years is a long time to perfect the art of jeans craftsmanship. Fortunately 1921 Premium Denim have mastered it and are now bringing their cult LA jeans to London. Denim brand fads are often more fleeting than runway trends themselves, but as one of the oldest family-owned denim manufactures in the world, heritage and endurance is something they clearly understand. Using Italian or Japanese denim, each piece is handcrafted, treated, washed and then finished with a special abrasion technique ensuring every pair is unique, and characterised by a vintage style finish. Not just lovingly crafted, but with a conscience too; all denim is spun from ecologically sound cottons. ■

SANDRA BACKLUND

Swedish knitwear genius Sandra Backlund incorporated human hair into her first collection of architectural, madcap knits. That phase has passed and she is now using only the richest red wools instead. A knitwear couturier, Backlund plays with structure, creating outlandish tulip skirts, massive shoulders and kooky headgear. Not a Puri knit in sight, thank God, just futuristic sculptures that manage to retain romance and femininity in their shapes. Her inventiveness has earnt her a place in knitting's renaissance. ■

BALENCIAGA

If the metal leggings are just a little too Tron for you, one can still indulge in Nicholas Ghesquière's feminine android futurism, with Balenciaga's first ever eyewear range. Echoing the space cadet look for his spring/summer 07 ready-to-wear collection, the eyewear line is a first for Ghesquière at the Parisian house.

Large transparent framed wraparounds, house grey or yellow reflective lenses with giant chrome studs on the arms. Cyber goggles they're not, not being bug-eyed has never been so chic.

Influenced heavily by sci-fi, this was Ghesquière's first full-on flirtation with the future - spurning plundering the archives of Cristobal like he's done in previous seasons. Decidedly creating his own legacy at Balenciaga, rather than just seizing the Spanish designers' radically formed silhouettes.

Think today, tomorrow, and what may be. Are the days of designers pilfering the past for inspiration gone? The future is now. ■

TOM FORD

The tanned Texan responsible for putting the sex back into Gucci is launching his first solo store in New York. 845 Madison Avenue, Manhattan is to be the home of the new TOM FORD signature menswear collection, which will include, RTW, footwear and eyewear. "My aim is to address an extremely discerning luxury customer who demands the highest quality product and service," claims Ford. Fortunately for disciples of his suave and polished chic, he's plans to spread his wings over the next few years - opening stores in Milan, London, LA and Tokyo. ■

EXPLOSIVE FASHION

ISSUE#1 SPRING 2007
£3.50 UK$9.99

WHEN JODIE MET AMANDA

A CONVERSATION WITH AMANDA LEPORE

Photograph **Ben Charles Edwards**
Words **Jodie Harsh**

I've known Amanda for a few years now. Before I met her for the first time I expected a terrifying diva, perhaps reminiscent of Pete Burns. In the flesh, away from the camp exaggerated images of her by LaChapelle, she is stunning. The moment I first met her, in an interview assignment for a magazine, my expectations were pleasantly shattered. When she answered the door to her hotel room in the East Village, NYC she came (no, she'd lived in for a decade with a big smile on her face and a kiss on the cheek, we bonded immediately over lipsticks and hairpieces.

What Amanda has done to her body and what I do to mine use two contrasting things. We both work in clubs and get paid to pull glamorous for the camera but I'm happy being a boy who dresses up for a living and for fun out for surreal reasons. Amanda, who has an often publicly flaunted vagina, was born Armand. She has used hormones, gender re-assignment surgery, cosmetic surgery, silicone injections, make-up and breast re-formation before she was 'Number One Transsexual in the World'. It, and deserves ultimate respect for it. There is quite possibly no-one else who has worked so much on their physical appearance and, boy, does this version work it..."

Grids: Creative Solutions for Graphic Designers

GRID SPECIFICATIONS

Page size (trimmed)	220 x 285mm
Top margin	15mm
Bottom margin	15mm
Outside margin	10mm
Inside margin	20mm
Number of columns	12
Gutter width	4mm
Extras	Baseline grid, 11pt

PLASTIQUE

Design: Matt Willey and Matt Curtis at Studio8 Design

Plastique is a quarterly women's fashion magazine. The basic elements of its design are very simple. There are two headline fonts; one text font, also used for the captions; and a 12-column grid that is frequently ignored! Designers Matt Willey and Matt Curtis wanted to work with as few rules as possible so that pages are designed as much through instinct as preconceived logic. The largely monochromatic color scheme was chosen to suit the ballsy and unapologetic nature of the magazine. As Willey says, "we didn't want anything too clinical, too fluffy, too saccharine, too girly."

GIL CARVALHO

"Never under estimate the power of the stiletto," says Gil Carvalho. Given that he's followed the career route of Mr Ford, who also gave up architecture for fashion design, Carvalho's ethos is on a par with his vigorous, towering platforms. Covered in vivid python and crocodile skins, with metallic leathers, they epitomize empowerment.

His architectural background is not entirely wasted however, like skyscrapers for the feet, Carvalho has produced a concept collection of soaring, polished steel stilettos – hand-laced elastic string, or satin cord that's woven to mould the foot – unmistakably requiring his construction precision and skill.

For something closer to the ground, Carvalho produces flat-of-foot sandals with slashed-leather fronts. Alternatively why not try his made-to-order black rubber and leather thigh-highs? ■

Todd Lynn is that kid at school that nobody noticed until parents' evening, where his mum and dad were unnecessarily cool as his report card gleamed, despite him being quiet, rebellious. With a bespoke-tailor CV reading like a rock 'n' roll-call of the last 40 years in music, it was no surprise his former mentor, Roland Mouret looked on admiringly in the front row. Lynn's collection was rife with androgynous tailoring – fluid lines that effortlessly sexed up waistcoats, tuxedo jackets, and cropped trousers, which were swapped between the girls and the boys. ■

TODD LYNN

ALEXANDER WANG

Thank goodness he left his San Francisco frat boy beginnings at the door when joining Marc Jacobs as an intern. It no doubt ensured that despite being only 23, his own collection is one of hot sophistication and understatement. Sticking with the cashmere roots planted in his very first 2004 collection with some tasty cardigans and sweaters. Wang also channelled his NYC street cred' via sporty playsuits and sexy micro shorts. Think Debbie Harry circa 1977. ■

MASTHEAD

JILLSTUART

CONTRIBUTORS

Grids: Creative Solutions for Graphic Designers

B1

GREAT EASTERN STREET

**PHOTOGRAPHY
DAVID DUNAN**

PAULE KA

OSMAN YOUSEFZADA

KIM JONES

LAGERFELD RANGE

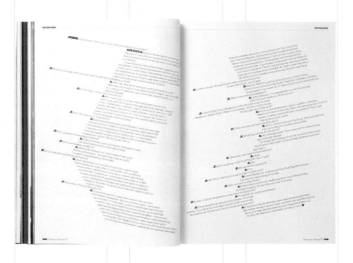

THE MAKING OF McQ

MYSPACE: CASTING AGENCY OF THE FUTURE?

Words Ellen Grace Jones
Photographs Alistair Allen

A MARRIAGE OF CULTURAL HISTORY & MODERN DESIGN

SEX DRUGS & TURKISH RUGS

Photo Kelly Carmichael

T

BOBS & BOY CUTS

THE SCISSORS ARE OUT AGAIN. THE BOB IS MOVING FORWARD INTO THE SPRING, REMAINING A STRONG TREND BUT WITH ADDED BITE. LOP A BIT MORE OFF AND GO WITH A BOY CUT

Photograph James Lloyd Evans

Grids: Creative Solutions for Graphic Designers

ZERO DEGREES
PHOTOGRAPHY JETTO GRAFSON

KILLAH KOLOR
PHOTOGRAPHY
JOHN LINDQUIST

AGGRESSORIES

**URBAN ARMOUR –
FASHIONISTAS ARM THEMSELVES FOR
EVERYDAY BATTLE**
Words: Ellen Grace Jones

DAY 2

DAY 3

ISSUE 2 SUMMER
LOOK OUT FOR IT

SUBSCRIBE NOW!

GO TO WWW.PLASTIQUEMAGAZINE.COM

**DRAGONETTE BRINGS PLASTIQUE
INTO THEIR WORLD OF ELECTRO-
POP ORGIES**

162_163

13.10.05
RIBA STIRLING
PRIZE

AJ

ISSN 0003-8466
£3.25

THE ARCHITECTS' JOURNAL WWW.AJPLUS.CO.UK

THE FASCINATION WITH
SURFACE GIVES THIS MOST
BASIC OF BUILDING TYPES
AN INTELLIGENCE AND
ENQUIRY THAT IS PALPABLE

1. Meeting
in defined by
overlapping volumes

Contents

P. 14
ZAHA HADID

P. 12
SAATCHI GALLERY

P. 25
TRANSPORT
INTERCHANGE

P. 46
JAN KAPLICKY

P. 58
TONY FRETTON

P. 16
MAKE

NEWS	AGENDA	BUILDING STUDY	TECHNICAL & PRACTICE	REVIEWS	REGULARS	JOBS & CLASSIFIED	AJPLUS.CO.UK
7	16–17	26–35	41–43	45	20	48	
11	18	36–37	44	47	22	55	
12–13				48	58		
14–15							

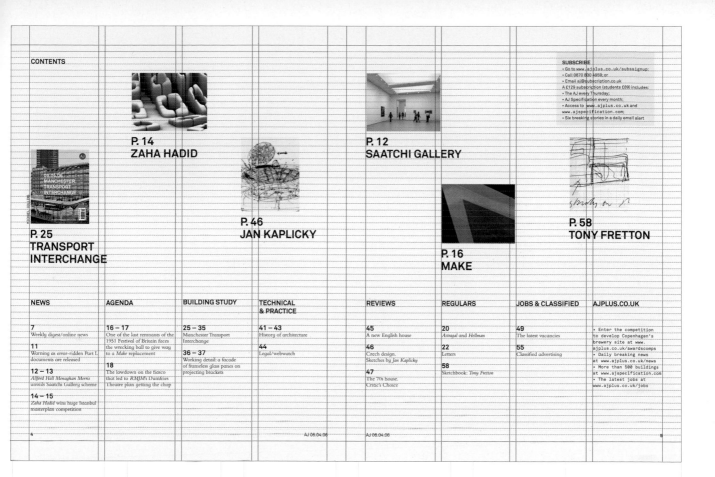

CONTENTS

P. 14
ZAHA HADID

P. 12
SAATCHI GALLERY

P. 25
TRANSPORT
INTERCHANGE

P. 46
JAN KAPLICKY

P. 16
MAKE

P. 58
TONY FRETTON

SUBSCRIBE
• Go to www.ajplus.co.uk/subssignup;
• Call 0870 830 4959; or
• Email aj@subscription.co.uk
A £129 subscription (students £89) includes:
• The AJ every Thursday;
• AJ Specification every month;
• Access to www.ajplus.co.uk and www.ajspecification.com;
• Six breaking stories in a daily email alert

NEWS	AGENDA	BUILDING STUDY	TECHNICAL & PRACTICE	REVIEWS	REGULARS	JOBS & CLASSIFIED	AJPLUS.CO.UK
7 Weekly digest/online news	16 – 17 One of the last remnants of the 1951 Festival of Britain faces the wrecking ball to give way to a *Make* replacement	25 – 35 Manchester Transport Interchange	41 – 43 History of architecture	45 A new English house	20 *Astragal* and *Hellman*	49 The latest vacancies	• Enter the competition to develop Copenhagen's brewery site at www.ajplus.co.uk/awardscomps
11 Warning as error-ridden Part L documents are released	18 The lowdown on the fiasco that led to RMJM's Dumfries Theatre plan getting the chop	36 – 37 Working detail: a facade of frameless glass panes on projecting brackets	44 Legal/webwatch	46 Czech design. Sketches by *Jan Kaplicky*	22 Letters	55 Classified advertising	• Daily breaking news at www.ajplus.co.uk/news
12 – 13 *Alford Hall Monaghan Morris* unveils Saatchi Gallery scheme				47 The 70s house. Critic's Choice	58 Sketchbook: *Tony Fretton*		• More than 500 buildings at www.ajspecification.com
14 – 15 *Zaha Hadid* wins huge Istanbul masterplan competition							• The latest jobs at www.ajplus.co.uk/jobs

4

AJ 06.04.06

AJ 06.04.06

5

GRID SPECIFICATIONS

Page size (trimmed)	210 x 265mm
Top margin	12mm
Bottom margin	12mm
Outside margin	12mm
Inside margin	12mm
Number of columns	4
Gutter width	4mm
Extras	Baseline grid, 3.883mm

AJ: THE ARCHITECTS' JOURNAL

Design: APFEL (A Practice for Everyday Life) with Sarah Douglas

APFEL redesigned *The Architects' Journal* in collaboration with Sarah Douglas. Together they developed a clean and simple design so that architectural process and progress are foregrounded. The grid is a simple four-column structure, and is used discreetly. Spreads look considered without being precious so that layouts can happily accommodate ephemeral content and at the same time showcase finished work. Images can be full bleed or squared up, and at times overlap or appear to hang from a top rule as though pinned on a wall. Folios, running feet, and rules at the top and bottom of each page quietly establish the overall page architecture.

Redefining Green-ness

Green-ness is the obscure object of desire that has been driving the development of suburbia since its beginnings. People fled to suburbia to get away from the congested city and its dense housing blocks, polluted air and car-dominated public space. The endless plains of fields and woods became a utopian image countering the urban dystopia of continuously built fabric. But as city dwellers started to migrate into suburbia, they brought with them their civilised baggage from the city and inevitably dumped it wherever they chose to settle anew. Hence the longing image of green landscape that was the reason for most suburbanites to come here in the first place was replaced over time, the difference being that people now had no other place left to go in order to find what they were looking for.

It is this paradox that the projects assembled here attempt to tackle. Common to all is the thesis that the degradation of landscape in suburbia is caused by a constant misunderstanding, and misuse, of green space. In today's suburbia, green space is, in fact, only very rarely staged to complement the built fabric with landscape. In most cases it serves a completely different objective, namely the provision of privacy. Hence the insurpassable importance of the front garden, which is basically a set-back space texture-mapped with green lawn.

To satisfy both desires, the schemes presented here propose to deal with them separately. Privacy, on the one hand, is achieved by raising the house in the air (Greenurbia) or sinking it in the ground (Sub-'burb), which in return frees up ground space for other uses, for instance public programmes. On the other hand, landscape is maintained by programming parts of the site with non-building programmes such as parks, gardens or agricultural uses (Fischbek-Mississippi) or by introducing a strong topographical definition (Sonic Polder).

DEEP PLANNING
West Side, New York

Ben Van Berkel and Caroline Bos have devised an urban strategy of 'deep planning', which responds to New York's needs as an unstable and mutating global city. This competition was sponsored by the oróck and included planning the West Side from 34th Street to 23rd Street. The metropolis is treated as a topology of fluctuating networks rather than distinct organisational units. Using combinations of temporal digital techniques, the project integrates infrastructure, urbanism and various programmes by looking for correspondences and overlaps between the locations and functions involved. The site is thus cast as a lobby for Manhattan, the aim being to respond to, rather than to dictate, patterns of use and function.

Due to their relatively short history there is less pressure on new interventions to comply with the piled-up fabric of the past

Redefining   Green-ness

Green-ness is the obscure object of desire that has been driving the development of suburbia since its beginnings. People fled to suburbia to get away from the congested city and its dense housing blocks, polluted air and car-dominated public space. The endless plains of fields and woods became a utopian image countering the urban dystopia of continuously built fabric. But as city dwellers started to migrate into suburbia, they brought with them their civilised baggage from the city and inevitably dumped it wherever they chose to settle anew. Hence the longing image of green landscape that was the reason for most suburbanites to come here in the first place was replaced over time, the difference being that people now had no other place left to go in order to find what they were looking for.

It is this paradox that the projects assembled here attempt to tackle. Common to all is the thesis that the degradation of landscape in suburbia is caused by a constant misunderstanding, and misuse, of green space. In today's suburbia, green space is, in fact, only very rarely staged to complement the built fabric with landscape. In most cases it serves a completely different objective, namely the provision of privacy. Hence the insurpassable importance of the front garden, which is basically a set-back space texture-mapped with green lawn.

To satisfy both desires, the schemes presented here propose to deal with them separately. Privacy, on the one hand, is achieved by raising the house in the air (Greenurbia) or sinking it in the ground (Sub-burb), which in return frees up ground space for other uses, for instance public programmes. On the other hand, landscape is maintained by programming parts of the site with non-building programmes such as parks, gardens or agricultural uses (Fischbek-Mississippi) or by introducing a strong topographical definition (Sonic Polder).

GRID SPECIFICATIONS

Page size (trimmed)	290 x 220mm
Top margin	25mm
Bottom margin	22mm
Outside margin	15mm
Inside margin	18mm
Number of columns	1, 2, or 4
Gutter width	4mm
Baseline grid	N/A

AD (ARCHITECTURAL DESIGN)

Design: Christian Küsters at CHK Design

Inspired by the Bauhaus, Christian Küsters took the "pure" forms of the square, the circle, and the triangle as his starting point in designing the AD logo. The redesign of the magazine grew out of this approach. The font usage and grid are part of a flexible template developed by Küsters to maximize variety in the content and reflect the different themes of each issue.

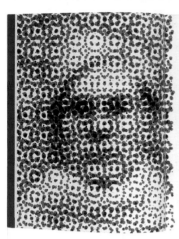

ART AND POLITICS

ROGER COOK

THE LOVE THAT DARES TO SPEAK ITS NAME

THE PRINCE

6

CHAPTER
—VI—

THE
PRINCE

CHAPTER VI

The drawing room of the Prince was hidden away beyond the great mail walls of the armoury, the entrance a secret doorway that sheltered behind the tapestry of the hunting unicorn. In a corner amongst the shadows of the dusty room, lined by the books of time sat an old withered man of leathersome visage, whose nostrils would flare at the fragrance of the dying sheets impregnating as many years decay into the remembrance of his walls. He was seated in front of his portrait, which hung on an easel half encrusted with a purple velvet throne. It had been painted as a portal, which in turn preserved the imposition of his soul. All of a sudden he drew himself up from his throne and declared to the room.

"I am the Prince of an ancient bloodline whose forefathers walked the path of the righteous through the valley of darkness. My species evolved through time by crafts of virtue, understanding the evolution of our inherited principalities of power. Mine is a kingdom not of this world", he paused licking his lips, the moves of which once systems history, and tasted the distinct flavour of nutmeg mixed with the metallic of blood, and with saliva running down his chin he spat out; "I do not fear, I do not love."

The elderly Prince sat back in his throne, his many children closely huddled beside him whispering in a rasping unison. Yet that is not deal that can eternal lie' and with long tongues they licked the wounds of his portrait that still wept from the scars of virtue and evil. The Prince had once woven the rich tapestry of shapes that had haunted all those that stood before him, for he was the keeper of the brotherhood and struck down with great vengeance and fury all those who attempted to poison or destroy. He knew the care of time was cracked and blackened, shrouded in scarlet rose, the stain of his sin. His physical and intellectual distinction was destined to continually bare witness to his fascination with rebellion, a charming disobedience that flirted with the inviting scar of evil. To be feared, or to be loved was the component of his cruelty.

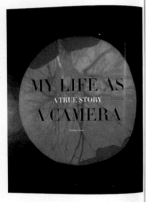

MY LIFE AS

A TRUE STORY

A CAMERA

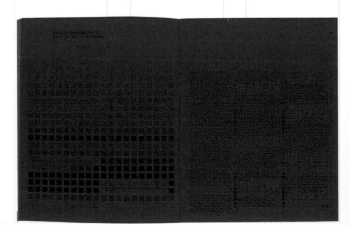

MERLIN JAMES

FICTIONS OF REPRESENTATION

The work of Merlin James (along with that of some of his near-contemporaries) offers an opportunity to examine some pressing issues within representational painting as perceived in the current climate of contemporary art. James's paintings are interesting because they appeal to some generality of perception of what a painting practice should be, while acknowledging a developmental modernist lineage, refuse to sit comfortably within this:

GRID SPECIFICATIONS

Page size (trimmed)	210 x 265mm
Top margin	18.8mm
Bottom margin	18.8mm
Outside margin	7.8mm
Inside margin	5.6mm
Number of columns	6
Gutter width	N/A
Extras	N/A

MISER & NOW

Design: Hannah Dumphy at CHK Design

Miser & Now (an anagram of the publishers' first names—Simon and Andrew) is an occasional visual arts magazine published by the Keith Talent Gallery. Art director Christian Küsters took banknote design as a starting point—a subliminal reminder of the relationship between the finance and fine art markets. Küsters and designer Hannah Dumphy respond to the editorial content of each issue and design accordingly—sometimes there isn't a conventional grid, sometimes each article is designed to fit its page using a flexible grid system, and sometimes opening pages are designed to read more like a poster.

Packaging

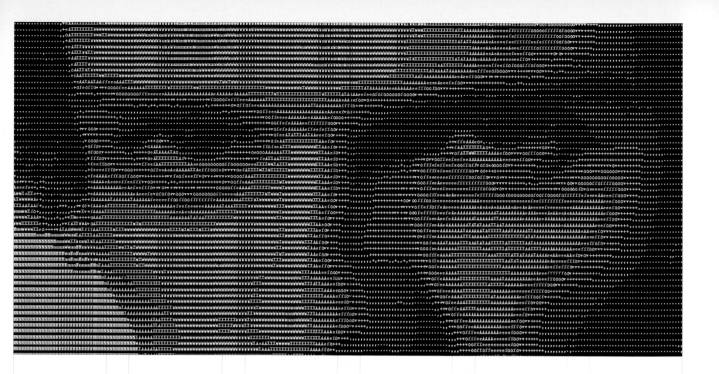

GRID SPECIFICATIONS

Page size (trimmed)	CD inlay: 150 x 117.5mm
	Booklet: 120.65 x 119.89mm
Top margin	N/A
Bottom margin	N/A
Outside margin	N/A
Inside margin	N/A
Number of columns	1
Gutter width	N/A
Extras	Baseline grid, as set by typewriter;
	56 horizontal rows

FREDDIE STEVENSON: A BODY ON THE LINE

Design: Rian Hughes at Device

Although the artwork was, in fact, put together on a Mac, with images created using an ASCII-art program, the overall impression of Rian Hughes' design for this CD packaging is that it is mechanically produced and generally low-tech. Hughes' intention was to echo Stevenson's music visually. Stevenson's music is made with little modern studio equipment, and without the aid of computer trickery. While there is no column grid employed, the type and images utilize a tightly packed series of horizontal lines that give a repetitive structure to the overall design, and increase its mechanical feel.

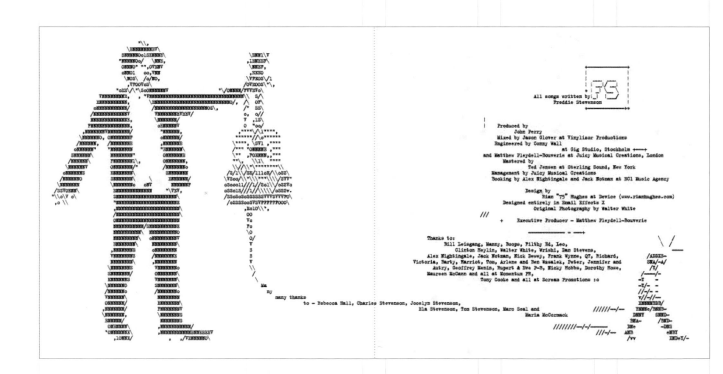

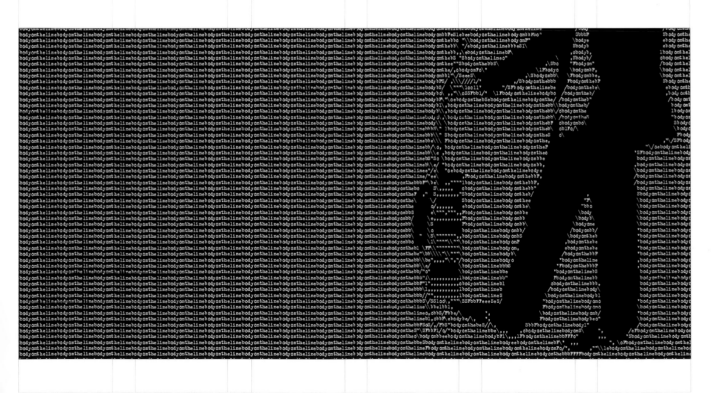

Adobe Systems Incorporated 2003 Annual Report

Adobe Systems Incorporated 2003 Annual Report

Adobe

GRID SPECIFICATIONS

Page size (trimmed)	256.1 x 359.8mm
Top margin	4.939mm
Bottom margin	4.233mm
Outside margin	4.939mm
Inside margin	12.7mm
Number of columns	2
Gutter width	4.233mm
Extras	N/A

ADOBE SYSTEMS INCORPORATED
2003 ANNUAL REPORT

*Design: Julian Bittiner and Brett Wickens
at MetaDesign San Francisco*

The brief for Adobe's 2003 Annual Report
was to highlight the company's heritage
and vision. With this in mind MetaDesign
created a brand framework around three
distinct themes: communicating ideas,
exchanging information, and sharing
memories. Once identified, these themes
determined the design, and MetaDesign
developed a simple, clear typographic and
photographic approach using a traditional
grid structure to underpin its modern-
looking designs.

Adobe Systems Incorporated Corporate overview

Adobe

Adobe Systems Incorporated Corporate overview

Adobe

GRID SPECIFICATIONS

Page size (trimmed)	260.35 x 378.9mm
Top margin	14.817mm
Bottom margin	21.167mm
Outside margin	14mm
Inside margin	14mm
Number of columns	3
Gutter width	4.233mm
Extras	N/A

**ADOBE SYSTEMS INCORPORATED
CORPORATE OVERVIEW**
*Design: Julian Bittiner at MetaDesign
San Francisco*

In this brochure, MetaDesign expanded
upon the themes of the Adobe Systems
2003 Annual Report (see pages 176_177).
The overall structure was similar, but
MetaDesign introduced bolder colors;
demonstrative photography, showing
how the applications are used; and large
typographic statements all designed to
convey the dynamism of the company and
reflect its leading brand position.

Adobe® Illustrator® CS2

Vector graphics reinvented

Illustrator® CS2

Adobe

Adobe

GRID SPECIFICATIONS

Page size (trimmed)	241 x 233mm
Top margin	8.46mm
Bottom margin	9.87mm
Outside margin	9mm
Inside margin	45mm
Number of columns	5
Gutter width	N/A
Extras	N/A

ADOBE ILLUSTRATOR CS2 PACKAGING

*Design: Hui-Ling Chen and Brett Wickens
at MetaDesign San Francisco*

In 2003, Adobe introduced the Creative
Suite and commissioned MetaDesign
to help it "emotionally reconnect" with
its graphically sophisticated audience by
redesigning the packaging and related
materials. Artist Nick Veasey, who works in
a studio specially equipped for radiography,
captured the X-rays used in the packaging
and icon system. These images reveal the
mathematical formulas that define many
forms found in nature—and are often used
by designers in developing geometric grid
structures. However, although the growth
pattern of a shell or the shape of a leaf
is determined by a fixed formula, no two
shells or leaves are exactly the same—
MetaDesign used this as a metaphor to
illustrate the variety of results possible
when using computer software.

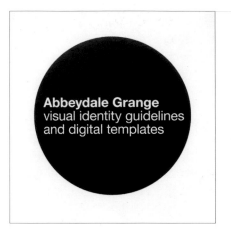

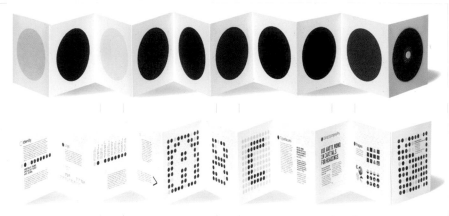

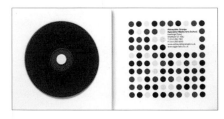

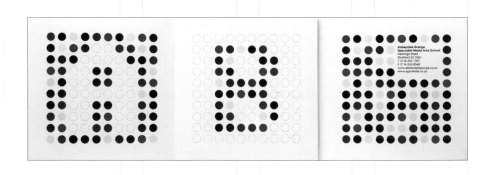

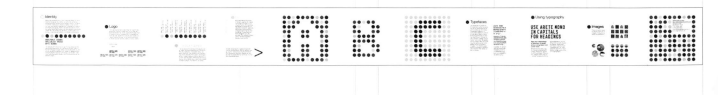

Grids: Creative Solutions for Graphic Designers

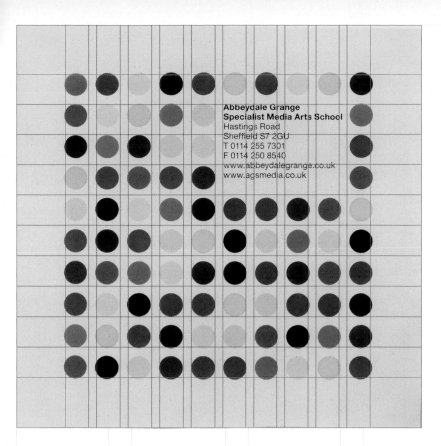

Abbeydale Grange
Specialist Media Arts School
Hastings Road
Sheffield S7 2GU
T 0114 255 7301
F 0114 250 8540
www.abbeydalegrange.co.uk
www.agsmedia.co.uk

GRID SPECIFICATIONS

Page size (trimmed)	1,763 x 160mm
Top margin	20mm
Bottom margin	20mm
Outside margin	20mm
Inside margin	20mm
Number of columns	140
Gutter width	3.131mm
Extras	10 horizontal fields

ABBEYDALE GRANGE IDENTITY

Design: Zoë Bather at Studio8 Design

Abbeydale is one of a number of schools that are involved in the Joinedupdesignforschools initiative run by the Sorrell Foundation. This initiative links designers with schools where the pupils are the commissioning clients. Working closely with the students, Studio8 developed a new visual identity for the school, creating a logo, stationery, signage, posters, brochures, and design guidelines to guarantee effective implementation of the identity. To ensure flexibility and consistency, designer Zoë Bather employed a multi-column structure, further divided into a series of small fields, across the various items. The school's vibrant multiculturalism—over 50 different languages are spoken there—is celebrated in the bright, multicolored graphics.

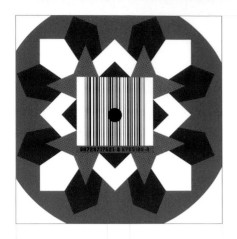

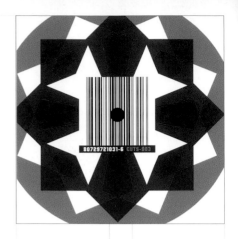

RAZ OHARA
HYMN MIXES

A1/JAHCOOZI REMIX //A2/RICHARD DAVIS REMIX //B1/RICHARD DAVIS ACID REPRISE //B2/LITWINENKO REMIX //33RPM

ALL TRACKS WRITTEN AND COMPOSED BY PATRICK RASMUSSEN/A1 REMIXED BY ROBOT KOCH/MIXED DOWN BY OREN GERLITZ AT JAHCOOZI STUDIO //A2 AND B1 REMIXES AND ADDITIONAL PRODUCTION BY RICHARD DAVIS /B 2 REMIX AND ADDITIONAL PRODUCTION BY LITWINENKO/ALL TRACKS PUBLISHED BY EDITION DIATHLON/BUDDE MUSIKVERLAG/MASTERED BY HELMUT ERLER AT DUBPLATES AND MASTERING/DESIGN BY ALORENZ BERLIN/MANUFACTURED BY HANDLE WITH CARE/WWW.HANDLEWITHCARE.DE/MADE IN GERMANY/BEMA/LC02916/P AND C 2005 KITTY-YO/WWW.KITTY-YO.COM/WORLDWIDE DISTRIBUTION BY INTERGROOVE/FAX 49(0)69-94547555/ORDER NO. CUTS-002-6/THIS IS SIDE B

CHIKINKI
ETHER RADIO REMIXES

A1/ETHER RADIO JAN DRIVER & SIR IUSMO – BOLT REMIX //A2/ASSASSINATOR 13 ED LALIQ'S ALBION CALL REMIX//B1/ETHER RADIO SERGE SANTIAGO VOCAL //45RPM

ALL TRACKS WRITTEN BY CHIKINKI/ COPYRIGHT CONTROL//A1 REMIX AND ADDITIONAL PRODUCTION BY JAN DRIVER AND SIRIUSMO/RECORDED AT THE SUPER-SOUND-SUITE BERLIN/JAN DRIVER APPEARS COURTESY OF BRAND PETROL RECORDINGS GERMANY/WWW.BRANDPETROL.INFO/A2 REMIX AND ADDITIONAL PRODUCTION BY E. KURDIS AND M. LANCASTER//B1 REMIX AND ADDITIONAL PRODUCTION BY SERGE SANTIAGO/MASTERED BY LUPO AT DUBPLATES AND MASTERING/DESIGN BY ALORENZ BERLIN/MANUFACTURED BY HANDLE WITH CARE/MADE IN GERMANY/BEMA/LC02916//A1 AND A2 P AND C 2005 KITTY-YO, THE KITTY-YO.COM//B1 P AND C 2004 AND 2005 UNIVERSAL ISLAND RECORDS LTD, UNDER EXCLUSIVE LICENSE TO KITTY-YO /WORLDWIDE DISTRIBUTION BY INTERGROOVE/FAX 49(0)69-94547555/ORDER NO. CUTS-001-6/THIS IS SIDE B

SEX IN DALLAS AND BILADOLL
GRAND OPENING EP

A1/GRAND OPENING //A2/THREADS //B1/THREADS KIDNAP'S PITCH BLACK LAKE MIX //B2/GRAND OPENING KONDYLOM REMIX BY GUITAR //33RPM

ALL TRACKS WRITTEN AND COMPOSED BY ADRIEN WALTER/MIA VON MATT/DAVID SUCARUDE/COPYRIGHT CONTROL//B1 ADDITIONAL REMIX PRODUCTION BY KIDNAP/THORSTEN SKINNING AND CORINNA VIDIC/WWW.THEKIDNAP.NET/B2 ADDITIONAL REMIX PRODUCTION BY GUITAR WHO APPEARS COURTESY OF CARELESS/ALL TRACKS RECORDED MIXED AND PRODUCED BY KIDNAP/A2 COPRODUCED BY SEX IN DALLAS AND BILADOLL/MASTERED BY ANDREAS AT SCHNITTSTELLE/DESIGN ALORENZ BERLIN/MANUFACTURED BY HANDLE WITH CARE/MADE IN GERMANY/BEMA/P AND C KITTY-CUTS 2005/WORLDWIDE DISTRIBUTION BY INTERGROOVE/FAX 0049(0)69-94 54 75 55/ORDER NO KY05100-6/THIS IS SIDE B

LITWINENKO
REISEFIEBER EP

A1/REISEFIEBER //B1/KAUBEAT //B2/OLTIMER //45RPM

ALL TRACKS WRITTEN BY LITWINENKO/TIMING MUSIC PUBLISHING/ARABELLA MUSIKVERLAG/MASTERED BY ANDREAS AT SCHNITTSTELLE /DESIGN ALORENZ BERLIN/MANUFACTURED BY HANDLE WITH CARE/MADE IN GERMANY/BEMA/P AND C KITTY-CUTS 2005/WORLDWIDE DISTRIBUTION BY INTERGROOVE/FAX 0049 (0) 69-94 54 75 55/ORDER NO KY05101-6/THIS IS SIDE B

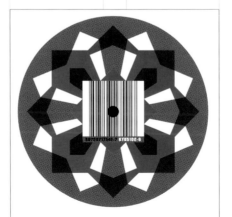

GOLD CHAINS & SUE CIE
CROWD CONTROL REMIXES

A1/CROWD CONTROL PHON.O REMIX //A2/CROWD CONTROL TOPHER LAFATA'S ALTERNATE VERSION //B1/CROWD CONTROL CB FUNK REMIX //33RPM

ALL TRACKS WRITTEN AND COMPOSED BY TOPHER LAFATA AND SUE COSTABILE /SEASIDE CITY MUSIC /A1 ADDITIONAL REMIX PRODUCTION BY PHON.O WHO APPEARS COURTESY OF SHITKATAPULT WWW.SHITKATAPULT.COM/A2 ADDITIONAL REMIX PRODUCTION BY TOPHER LA FATA//B1 ADDITIONAL REMIX PRODUCTION EB FUNK WHO APPEARS COURTESY OF PUNKT MUSIC /PRODUCED BY TOPHER LA FATA /VLADISLAV DELAY/SUE COSTABILE/RECORDED AT ZOMBIE STUDIOS SAN FRANCISCO BY OCSC/MIXED BY VLADISLAV DELAY AND TOPHER LAFATA AT BASSDROSS BERLIN/MASTERED BY ANDREAS AT SCHNITTSTELLE/DESIGN ALORENZ BERLIN/MANUFACTURED BY HANDLE WITH CARE/MADE IN GERMANY/BEMA/UNDER EXCLUSIV LICENSE BY KILL ROCK STARS /KILL ROCK STARS C KITTY-CUTS 2005/WORLDWIDE DISTRIBUTION BY INTERGROOVE/FAX 49 (0) 69-94 54 75 55/ORDER NO KY05102-6/SIDE B

KITTY CUTS

Design: Angela Lorenz at
alorenz, Berlin/Wien

Taking the name of the series at face value (in German "cut" is "Schnitt" and "intersection" is "Schnittmenge"), Angela Lorenz constructed the design for these 12in EP labels by appearing to cut into the central square that holds the bar code. Rotating, enlarging, and repeating this shape along its diagonal forms a star shape that resembles images created by a kaleidoscope or the cut of a jewel. Although Lorenz isn't working with a traditional horizontal/ vertical grid, the resulting forms are repetitive and geometrically derived.

GRID SPECIFICATIONS

Page size (trimmed)	100 x 100mm
Top margin	To bleed
Bottom margin	To bleed
Outside margin	To bleed
Inside margin	To bleed
Number of columns	N/A
Gutter width	N/A
Extras	Grid developed from base unit— 32mm square

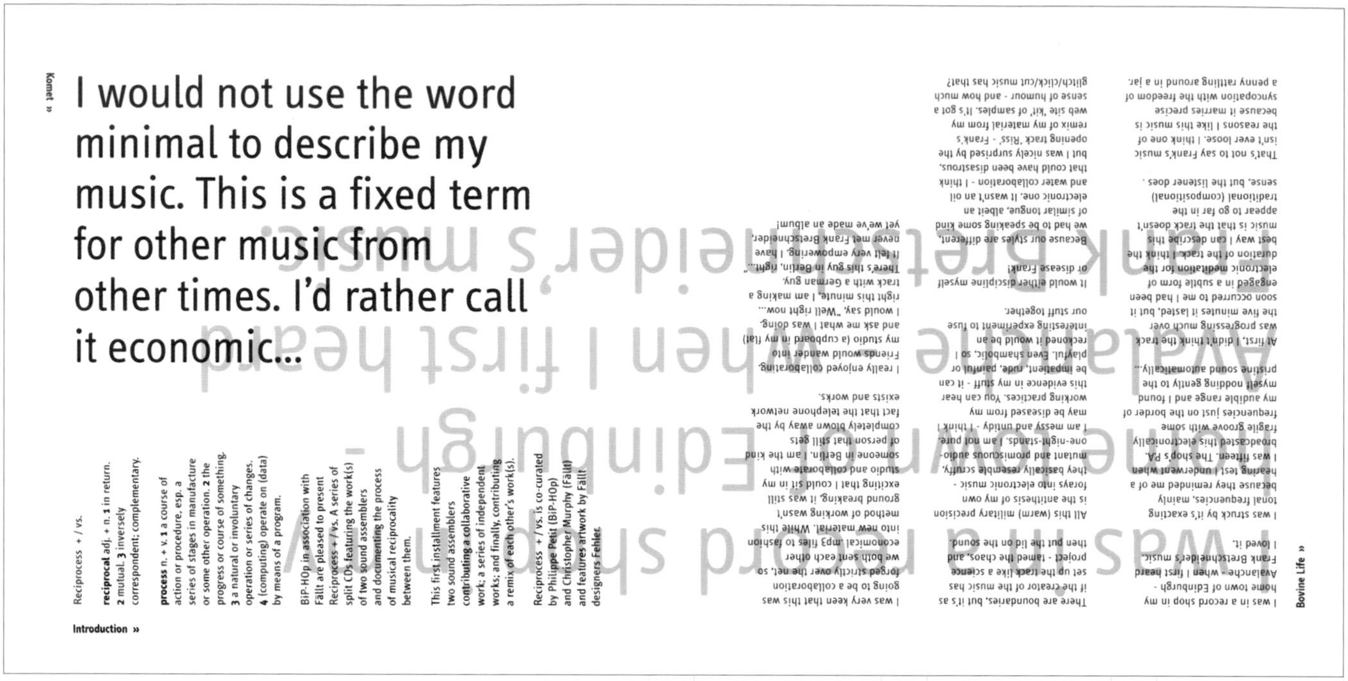

I would not use the word minimal to describe my music. This is a fixed term for other music from other times. I'd rather call it economic...

Reciprocess · + / vs.

reciprocal adj. + n. 2 in return. 2 mutual. 3 inversely correspondent; complementary.

process n. – v.1 a course of action or procedure, esp. a series of stages in manufacture or some other operation. 2 the progress or course of something. 3 a natural or involuntary operation or series of changes. 4 (computing) operate on (data) by means of a program.

BIP-HOp is pleased to present Reciprocess + / vs. A series of split CDs featuring the work(s) of two sound assemblers and documenting the process of musical reciprocality between them.

This first installment features two sound assemblers contributing a collaborative work, a series of independent works; and finally, contributing a remix of each other's work(s).

Reciprocess + / vs. is co-curated by Philippe Petit (BIP-HOp) and Christopher Murphy (Fällt) and features artwork by Fällt designers Fehler.

(rotated text, right page)

glitch/click/cut music has that?

This is not to say Frank's music isn't ever loose. I think one of the reasons I like this music is because it marries precise syncopation with the freedom of a penny rattling around in a jar.

That's not to say Frank's music isn't ever loose. I think one of the reasons I like this music is because it marries precise syncopation with the freedom of a penny rattling around in a jar.

Because our styles are different, we had to be speaking some kind of similar tongue, albeit an electronic one. It wasn't an oil and water collaboration – I think yet we've made an album!

I really enjoyed collaborating. Friends would wander into my studio's cupboard in my flat! It felt very empowering, I have never met Frank Bretschneider.

There's this guy in Berlin, right? I would say, "Well right now... and ask me what I was doing. right this minute, I am making a track with a German guy, someone in Berlin, I am the kind of person that still gets completely blown away by the fact that the telephone network exists and works.

It would either discipline myself or disease Frank!

All this (warm) military precision is the antithesis of my own forays into electronic music – they basically resemble scruffy, mutant and promiscuous audio-one-night-stands. I am not pure, I am messy and unruly – I think I may be diseased from my working practices. You can hear this evidence in my stuff – it can be impatient, rude, painful or playful. Even shambolic, so I reckoned it would be an interesting experiment to fuse our stuff together.

At first, I didn't think the track soon occurred to me. I had been engaged in a subtle form of electronic meditation for the best way I can describe this music is that the track doesn't appear to go far in the duration of the track! I think the pristine sound automatically.

There are boundaries, but it's as if the creator of the music has set up the track like a science project – tamed the chaos, and then put the lid on the sound.

I was in a record shop in my home town of Edinburgh – Avalanche – when I first heard Frank Bretschneider's music.

(Second spread, left page)

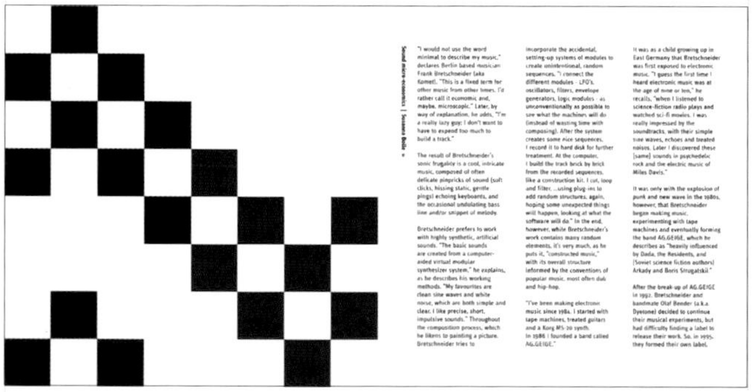

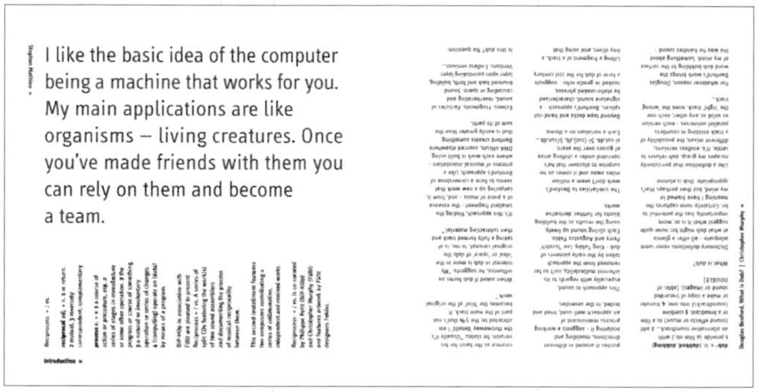

I like the basic idea of the computer being a machine that works for you. My main applications are like organisms – living creatures. Once you've made friends with them you can rely on them and become a team.

(Third spread, left page - rotated)

I like precise impulsive sounds, sine waves and white noise, which are both simple and clear.

I'm a bit uncontrolled and easily distracted, but this allows my compositions to be guided by the circumstances of the moment.

(Third spread, right page - rotated)

I have a constant impatience with my own sound, seeking to devolve and simplify it, whilst leaving an emotional content.

I would not use the word minimal to describe my music. This is a fixed term for other music from other times. I'd rather call it economic...

GRID SPECIFICATIONS

Page size (trimmed)	120 x 120mm
Top margin	12mm
Bottom margin	12mm
Outside margin	12mm
Inside margin	12mm
Number of columns	3
Gutter width	6mm
Extras	Baseline grid, 12.7mm; 3 horizontal fields

+/VS.

Design: Fehler

This series of CDs features soundworks by two different artists. Each contributes solo tracks as well as remixing the other's work, so the brief was to create a design that didn't privilege one artist over the other. A democratic solution was achieved by creating a grid that reads in four directions: right side up for one artist, right side down for the other, with the other two axes left to hold commentary and essays.

Posters & fliers

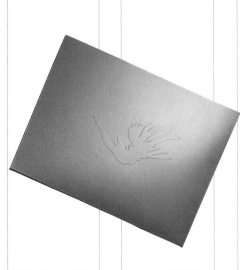

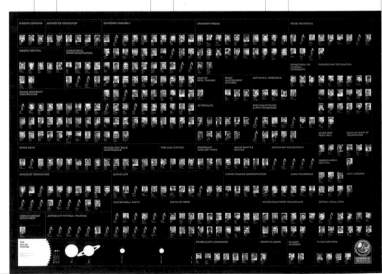

GRID SPECIFICATIONS

Page size (trimmed)	100 x 700mm
Top margin	21mm
Bottom margin	21mm
Outside margin	21mm
Inside margin	21mm
Number of columns	38
Gutter width	37mm
Extras	Front: 10 horizontal fields
	Back: 17 horizontal fields

SUNSHINE

Design: Airside

This foldout double-sided poster was designed for DNA Films as
a gift for the crew involved in making the movie *Sunshine*. The back
of the poster shows the crew listed as though members of a space
mission. The grid wasn't determined by content and page size alone.
It was planned so that images of over 400 crew members, and all
relevant information, would fit on one side of the poster without any
picture or text running over the three folds.

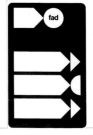

GRID SPECIFICATIONS

Page size (trimmed)	Resizable, as required
Top margin	1 base unit
Bottom margin	1 base unit
Outside margin	1 base unit
Inside margin	1 base unit
Number of columns	Flexible
Gutter width	1 base unit
Extras	Grid developed from base unit—square

FAD GRAPHIC GUIDELINE

Design: BaseDESIGN

Three basic shapes—the square, the triangle, and the circle—form the core of the graphic system of BaseDESIGN's identity for FAD, a Spanish, not-for-profit cultural body promoting design, architecture, and art. The grid is determined by multiples of these forms, creating vertical and horizontal bands across the page. These bands are then used as columns and fields would be in a conventional grid.

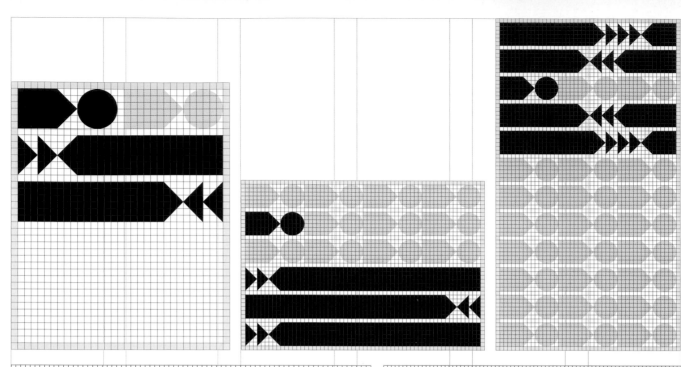

»Exhibition Convent dels Angels August 2006 ‹‹

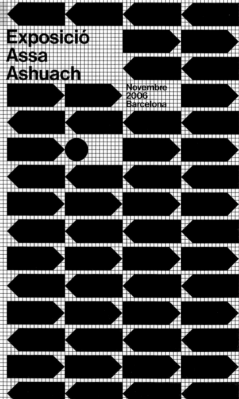

Exposició Assa Ashuach

Novembre 2006 Barcelona

Grids: Creative Solutions for Graphic Designers

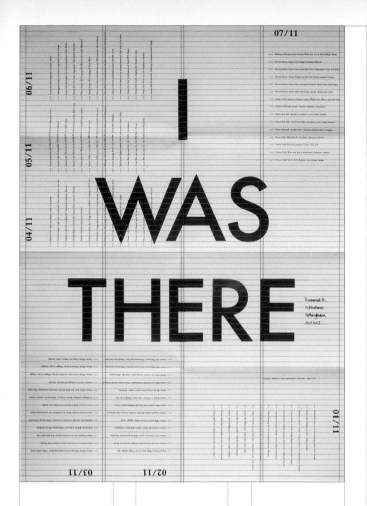

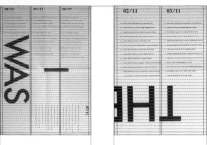

PERSONAL PROJECT

Design: George Adams

This is a personal project documenting a week in the life of designer George Adams. Every hour of the day is represented typographically, using categories such as "my location" and "my last conversation" to help the viewer navigate the piece. Adams was interested in how standard A paper sizes could be divided into areas that would represent units of time. When folded down to A4 (210 x 297mm [c. 8⅛ x 11⅝in]), only the first day is visible—the full week is revealed when the sheet is opened out to A1 (594 x 841mm [c. 23½ x 33in]).

GRID SPECIFICATIONS

Page size (trimmed)	A1 (594 x 841mm [c. 23½ x 33in]) folded down to A4 (210 x 297mm [c. 8⅛ x 11⅝in])
Top margin	All sheets: 10mm
Bottom margin	All sheets: 10mm
Outside margin	A1, A2, and A3: 10mm/A4: 70mm
Inside margin	All sheets: 10mm
Number of columns	A1: 4/A2: 3/A3: 2/A4: 1
Gutter width	5mm
Extras	Baseline grid, 10mm

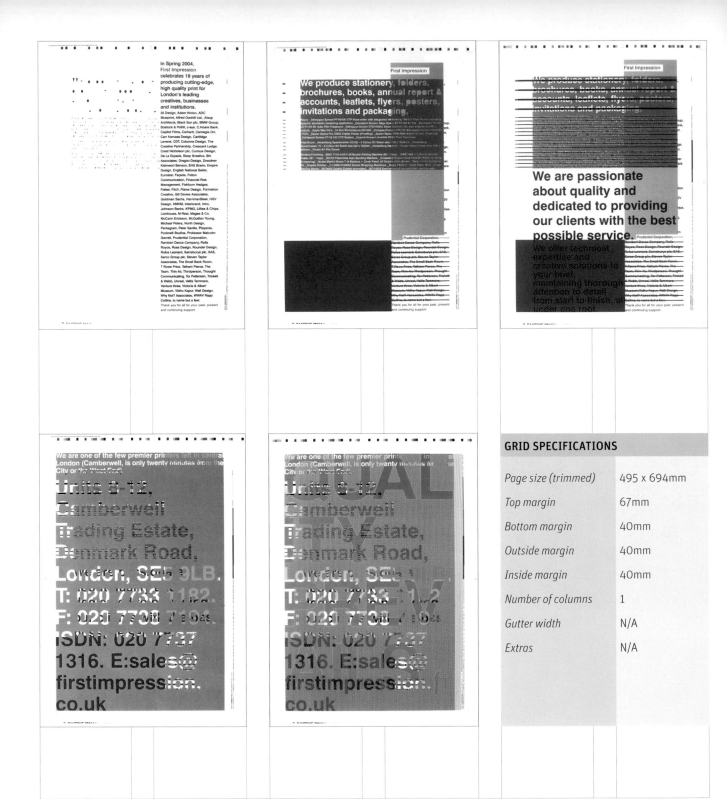

GRID SPECIFICATIONS

Page size (trimmed)	495 x 694mm
Top margin	67mm
Bottom margin	40mm
Outside margin	40mm
Inside margin	40mm
Number of columns	1
Gutter width	N/A
Extras	N/A

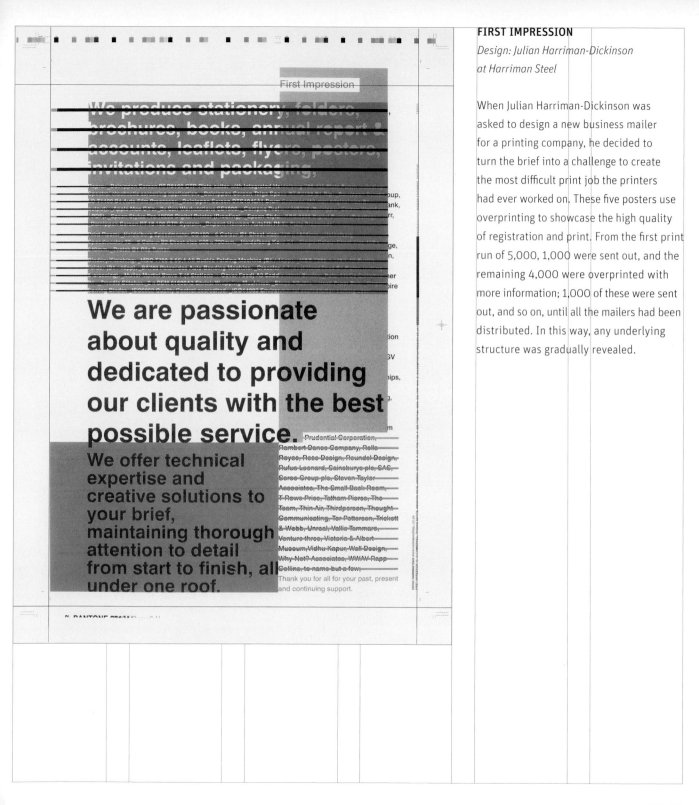

First Impression

We produce stationery, folders, brochures, books, annual report & accounts, leaflets, flyers, posters, invitations and packaging,

We are passionate about quality and dedicated to providing our clients with the best possible service. We offer technical expertise and creative solutions to your brief, maintaining thorough attention to detail from start to finish, all under one roof.

When Julian Harriman-Dickinson was asked to design a new business mailer for a printing company, he decided to turn the brief into a challenge to create the most difficult print job the printers had ever worked on. These five posters use overprinting to showcase the high quality of registration and print. From the first print run of 5,000, 1,000 were sent out, and the remaining 4,000 were overprinted with more information; 1,000 of these were sent out, and so on, until all the mailers had been distributed. In this way, any underlying structure was gradually revealed.

Luke Wood is the
Head of Design at
the University of
Canterbury and a
practising designer.
He designed and
exhibited a typeface
replicating the script of
Colin McCahon's word
paintings, and recently
held a residency at
Hatch Show Prints in
Nashville.

Hamish Thompson
is the author and
designer of Paste-up:
A Century of New
Zealand Poster Art.
Trained at the Basel
School of Design
in Switzerland, he
has taught, written
about and practised
design for over
20 years.

Catherine Griffiths
is an innovative
typographer who
designed the BEST
Design Award-winning
Wellington Writers
Walk and gave a new
meaning to concrete
poetry. Design from
her Wellington studio,
Epitome, spans print
and architecture.

OLD SCHOOL

NEW SCHOOL

TRUETYPE SCHOOL

3 DESIGNERS SPEAK

Hamish Thompson 'Poster Design'
Mon 15 Aug 12-1pm
St David 1

Catherine, Hamish & Luke Tues 16
Open Lecture Aug 6.30pm
Archway 3

Catherine & Luke 'Design & Typography'
seminar Wed 17 Aug 1-2pm
Design Studies CApSc 1.05

Brought to you by:

New Zealand Print Culture Area of Research Strength

DINZ (Designers Institute of New Zealand)

Design Studies | Te Toki a Rata

OTAGO

OLD SCHOOL

NEW SCHOOL

TRUETYPE SCHOOL

3 DESIGNERS SPEAK

GRID SPECIFICATIONS

Page size (trimmed)	400 x 600mm
Top margin	N/A
Bottom margin	N/A
Outside margin	N/A
Inside margin	50mm
Number of columns	8
Gutter width	N/A
Extras	Grid developed from base unit— rectangle with ratio of 2:3; baseline grid, 22pt; 8 horizontal fields

OLD SCHOOL, NEW SCHOOL, TRUETYPE SCHOOL

Design: Lightship Visual

This poster was designed for a series of graphic design lectures at the University of Otago, New Zealand. The surface area of the poster is divided to form eight vertical and eight horizontal fields. The gray background provides a neutral ground for colored rectangular panels that correspond with this underlying system of organization and draw attention to the poster's structure. Designer Stuart Medley's decision to foreground the grid as an organizing principle was informed by the panel of speakers, which included designers taught by Emil Ruder and Wolfgang Weingart.

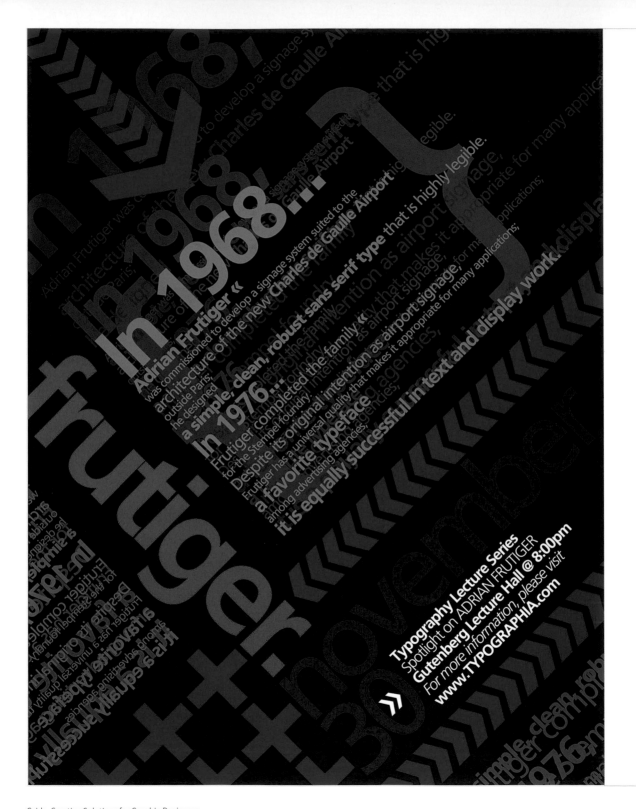

In 1968, Adrian Frutiger was commissioned to develop a signage system suited to the architecture of the new Charles de Gaulle Airport outside Paris. In 1976, he designed a simple, clean, robust sans serif type that is highly legible. Frutiger completed the family for the Stempel foundry. Despite its original intention as airport signage, Frutiger has a universal quality that makes it appropriate for many applications; a favorite typeface among advertising agencies, it is equally successful in text and display work.

Typography Lecture Series
Spotlight on ADRIAN FRUTIGER
Gutenberg Lecture Hall @ 8:00pm
For more information, please visit
www.TYPOGRAPHIA.com

30 november

GRID SPECIFICATIONS

Page size (trimmed)	457.2 x 609.6mm
Top margin	To bleed
Bottom margin	To bleed
Outside margin	To bleed
Inside margin	To bleed
Number of columns	11
Column gutter	N/A
Extras	rotated grid;
	8 horizontal fields

FRUTIGER POSTER

Design: Reggie Hidalgo at
The Art Institute of California

This poster promotes a lecture series on typography, in particular, the work of Adrian Frutiger. It uses a series of angled alignments. The poster is divided into 11 columns and eight horizontal fields. Although this isn't a conventional grid, composed of equal columns or fields and gutters, it is reminiscent of the organizational approach followed by exponents of the Swiss school in the design of posters. Using these methods, art director Maggie Rossoni and designer Reggie Hidalgo have created a dynamic piece of design information that is easy to navigate.

tHE
BABYSHAMBLES SESSiONS
1, 2 & 3

available for download from : http://www.babyshambles.net

...at the end of his tether., Barât quit the version halfway through. Doherty, true to form, made the abandoned demos available for free on the internet, calling them The Babyshambles Sessions.

THE BABYSHAMBLES SESSIONS 1, 2 & 3

available for download from : http : www.babyshambles.net

...at the end of his tether. Barât quit the session halfway through. Doherty, true to form, made the abandoned demos available for free on the internet, calling them The Babyshambles Sessions.

GRID SPECIFICATIONS

Page size (trimmed)	580 x 990mm
Top margin	170mm
Bottom margin	20mm
Outside margin	30mm
Inside margin	40mm
Number of columns	26
Gutter width	N/A
Extras	40 horizontal rows

BABYSHAMBLES SESSIONS
Design: Peter Crnokrak at ±

The Babyshambles Sessions are a series of studio sessions by The Libertines recorded a few months before their breakup and made available as free downloads by Pete Doherty. This promotional poster prototype features a grid of 3,050 1 x 1cm squares—each hand-colored using Pantone Tria markers on Lambda Duraflex—that make up an image of Doherty's face. Designer Peter Crnokrak wanted the hand-colored squares to communicate the contrast between the digital medium of the sessions and the lo-fi acoustic content of the music.

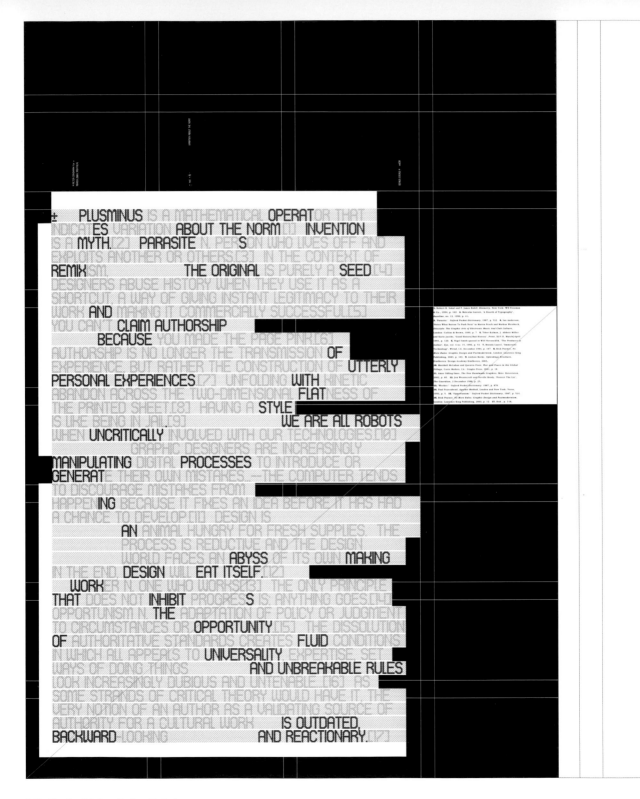

± PLUSMINUS IS A MATHEMATICAL OPERATOR THAT INDICATES VARIATION ABOUT THE NORM [1] INVENTION IS A MYTH. [2] PARASITE N. PERSON WHO LIVES OFF AND EXPLOITS ANOTHER OR OTHERS [3] IN THE CONTEXT OF REMIXISM, THE ORIGINAL IS PURELY A SEED [4] DESIGNERS ABUSE HISTORY WHEN THEY USE IT AS A SHORTCUT, A WAY OF GIVING INSTANT LEGITIMACY TO THEIR WORK AND MAKING IT COMMERCIALLY SUCCESSFUL [5] YOU CAN'T CLAIM AUTHORSHIP BECAUSE YOU MADE THE PAGE PINK [6] AUTHORSHIP IS NO LONGER THE TRANSMISSION OF EXPERIENCE BUT RATHER THE CONSTRUCTION OF UTTERLY PERSONAL EXPERIENCES [7] UNFOLDING WITH KINETIC ABANDON ACROSS THE TWO-DIMENSIONAL FLATNESS OF THE PRINTED SHEET [8] HAVING A STYLE IS LIKE BEING IN JAIL. [9] WE ARE ALL ROBOTS WHEN UNCRITICALLY INVOLVED WITH OUR TECHNOLOGIES. [10] GRAPHIC DESIGNERS ARE INCREASINGLY MANIPULATING DIGITAL PROCESSES TO INTRODUCE OR GENERATE THEIR OWN MISTAKES —THE COMPUTER TENDS TO DISCOURAGE MISTAKES FROM HAPPENING BECAUSE IT FIXES AN IDEA BEFORE IT HAS HAD A CHANCE TO DEVELOP. [11] DESIGN IS AN ANIMAL HUNGRY FOR FRESH SUPPLIES. THE PROCESS IS REDUCTIVE AND THE DESIGN WORLD FACES AN ABYSS OF ITS OWN MAKING IN THE END DESIGN WILL EAT ITSELF. [12] WORKER N. ONE WHO WORKS [13] THE ONLY PRINCIPLE THAT DOES NOT INHIBIT PROGRESS IS ANYTHING GOES. [14] OPPORTUNISM IN THE ADAPTATION OF POLICY OR JUDGMENT TO CIRCUMSTANCES OR OPPORTUNITY [15] THE DISSOLUTION OF AUTHORITATIVE STANDARDS CREATES FLUID CONDITIONS IN WHICH ALL APPEALS TO UNIVERSALITY EXPERTISE SET WAYS OF DOING THINGS AND UNBREAKABLE RULES LOOK INCREASINGLY DUBIOUS AND UNTENABLE [16] AS SOME STRANDS OF CRITICAL THEORY WOULD HAVE IT, THE VERY NOTION OF AN AUTHOR AS A VALIDATING SOURCE OF AUTHORITY FOR A CULTURAL WORK IS OUTDATED, BACKWARD-LOOKING AND REACTIONARY. [17]

1. Robert B. Sokol and F. James Rohlf, Biometry, New York, WH Freeman & Co., 1994, p. 163. 2. Malcolm Garrett, 'A Dearth of Typography' Baseline, no. 13, 1990, p. 41.
3. 'Parasite,' Oxford Pocket Dictionary, 1987, p. 552. 4. Ian Anderson, 'Remix What Button To Push Now' in Marvin Poetz and Nathan Woodrich, Disciple: The Graphic Arts of Electronic Music And Club Culture, London: Collins & Brown, 1999, p. 7. 5. Tibor Kalman, J. Abbott Miller and Karrie Jacobs, 'Good History/Bad History', Print, XLV:II, March/April 1991, p. 120. 6. Nigel Smith quoted in Will Novosedlik, 'The Producer as Author', Eye, vol. 4 no. 15, 1994, p. 51. 7. Brenda Laurel, 'Innercraft Technology' Wired, 1.6, December 1993, p. 107. 8. Rick Poynor, No More Rules: Graphic Design and Postmodernism, London: Laurence King Publishing, 2003, p. 103. 9. Jochen Reider, Iglooteign, Brochure, Eindhoven: Design Academy Eindhoven, 2003.
10. Marshall McLuhan and Quentin Fiore, War and Peace in the Global Village, Corte Madera, CA: Gingko Press, 2001, p. 10.
11. Anne Odling-Smee, The New Handmade Graphics, Mies: Rotovision, 2002, p. 87. 12. Jon Wozencroft and Neville Brody, 'Protect The Lie', The Guardian, 2 December 1988, p. 25.
13. 'Worker,' Oxford Pocket Dictionary, 1987, p. 870.
14. Paul Feyerabend, Against Method, London and New York: Verso, 1993, p. 9. 15. 'Opportunism,' Oxford Pocket Dictionary, 1987, p. 574.
16. Rick Poynor, No More Rules: Graphic Design and Postmodernism, London: Laurence King Publishing, 2003, p. 13. 17. Ibid., p. 116.

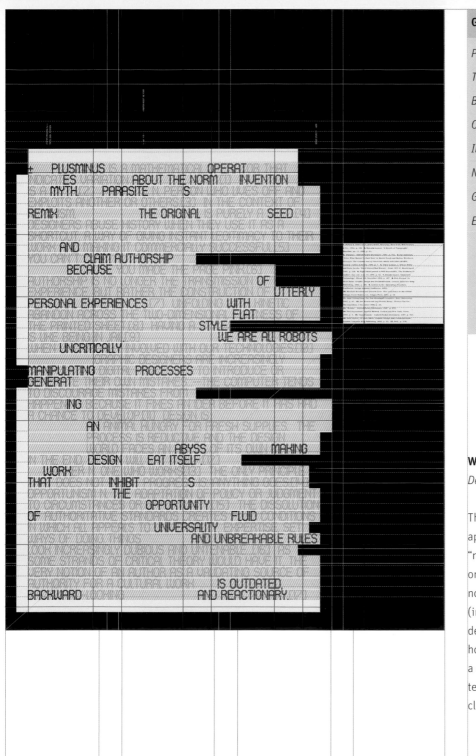

GRID SPECIFICATIONS

Page size (trimmed)	840 x 1,170mm
Top margin	193mm
Bottom margin	41mm
Outside margin	154mm
Inside margin	49mm
Number of columns	4
Gutter width	N/A
Extras	8 horizontal fields, 6 lines per field

WORKER/PARASITE MANIFESTO

Design: Peter Crnokrak at ±

The ± worker/parasite manifesto uses appropriated statements and graphics "remixed" by designer Peter Crnokrak. The original quotes all relate in some form to notions of originality, authorship, and rules (including the use of the grid) in graphic design. These are printed in light-gray horizontal lines that can only be read from a certain distance, while the ± manifesto text is highlighted in black, thereby making clear what is a paradox for Crnokrak.

love will tear us apart
again.

love will tear us apart again.

GRID SPECIFICATIONS

Page size (trimmed)	594 x 841mm
Top margin	27.5mm
Bottom margin	9.7mm
Outside margin	9.7mm
Inside margin	9.7mm
Number of columns	N/A
Gutter width	N/A
Extras	N/A

LOVE WILL TEAR US APART AGAIN

Design: Peter Crnokrak at ±

This poster uses the principles of information design to compare over 85 cover versions of Joy Division's "Love Will Tear Us Apart Again." Each version is mapped to show how long after the original it was recorded, along with the recording artist, release name and date, and label. The design uses the visually seductive device of lines radiating from a circle to structure the information. The print on off-white, heavy-weight art paper is a nod to the original graphic material produced for Joy Division by designer Peter Saville.

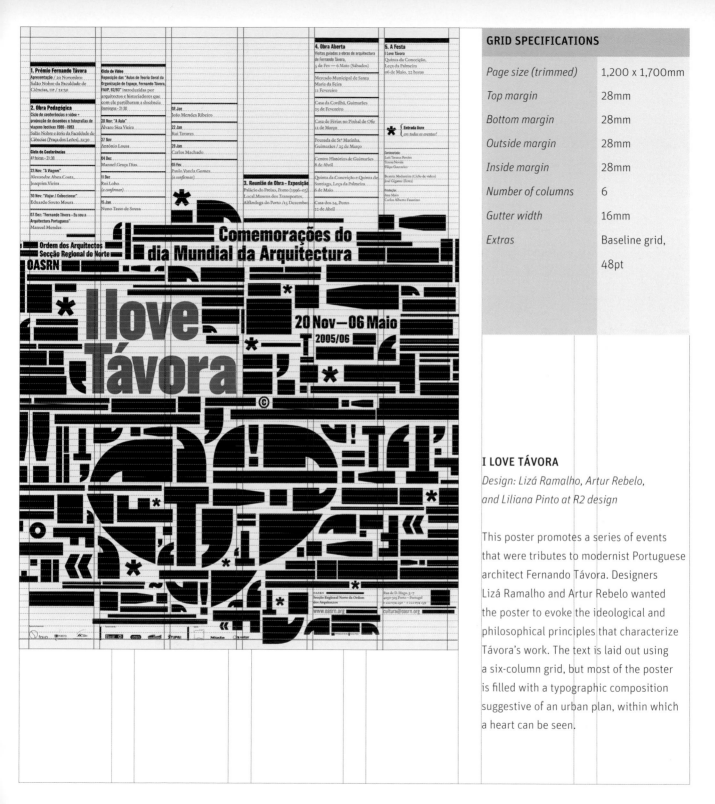

GRID SPECIFICATIONS

Page size (trimmed)	1,200 x 1,700mm
Top margin	28mm
Bottom margin	28mm
Outside margin	28mm
Inside margin	28mm
Number of columns	6
Gutter width	16mm
Extras	Baseline grid, 48pt

I LOVE TÁVORA

Design: Lizá Ramalho, Artur Rebelo, and Liliana Pinto at R2 design

This poster promotes a series of events that were tributes to modernist Portuguese architect Fernando Távora. Designers Lizá Ramalho and Artur Rebelo wanted the poster to evoke the ideological and philosophical principles that characterize Távora's work. The text is laid out using a six-column grid, but most of the poster is filled with a typographic composition suggestive of an urban plan, within which a heart can be seen.

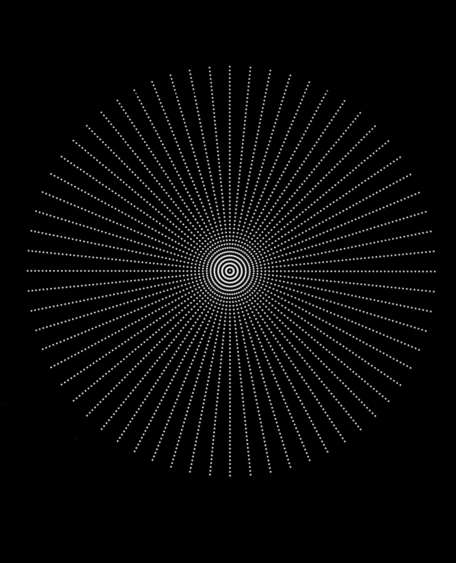

ON/OFF

A Sound Seminar Thursday 15th December 6pm RCafé

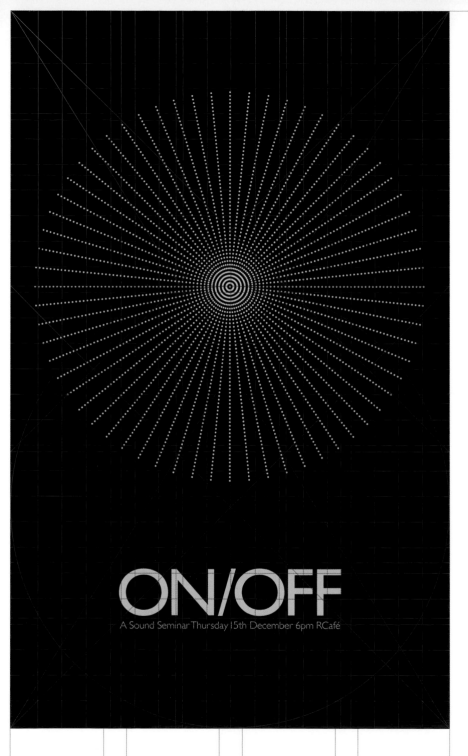

GRID SPECIFICATIONS

Page size (trimmed)	512 x 832mm
Top margin	32mm
Bottom margin	32mm
Outside margin	32mm
Inside margin	32mm
Number of columns	16
Gutter width	N/A
Extras	Baseline grid, 3.2mm; 28 fields

ON/OFF

Design: Richard Sarson

This poster advertised a series of seminars on sound that were held at the Royal College of Art, London, where Richard Sarson was a student. Inspired by Josef Müller-Brockmann and Jan Tschichold, Sarson used abstract shapes to explore visual representations of rhythm and sound, and looked to geometry to develop his grid by taking the golden section as his starting point.

GRID SPECIFICATIONS

Page size (trimmed)	700 x 1,000mm
Top margin	To bleed
Bottom margin	To bleed
Outside margin	To bleed
Inside margin	To bleed
Number of columns	34
Gutter width	N/A
Extras	Grid developed from base unit—portrait rectangle

ROTARY CLUB PHILHARMONIC CONCERT
Design: Boris Ljubicic at Studio International

Designer Boris Ljubicic's creative inspiration for this concert poster was the three-tonal scale of the music. The poster is divided into a grid of narrow columns and fields, each filled with an image to form a mosaic of photographs—a visual representation of the rich orchestral music to be played at the concert. Ljubicic describes the process of importing these images into the grid as similar to composing virtual music.

CROATIA   The Mediterranean as it once was

GRID SPECIFICATIONS

Page size (trimmed)	1,400 x 1,000mm
Top margin	To bleed
Bottom margin	To bleed
Outside margin	To bleed
Inside margin	To bleed
Number of columns	16; 8 per image
Gutter width	N/A
Extras	Grid is broken along vertical columns to intersperse two separate images

CROATIA   The Mediterranean as it once was

3-D POSTERS

Design: Boris Ljubicic at Studio International

Boris Ljubicic's intention in designing these posters for the Croatian National Tourist Board was to provide a contrast to the conventional photographic poster aimed at vacationers. These posters are three dimensional, with the folds forming the grid. Photographs of traditional tourist sites are juxtaposed with images of tourists themselves in order to encourage viewer curiosity and participation. When viewed from different angles, the posters show an alternative image.

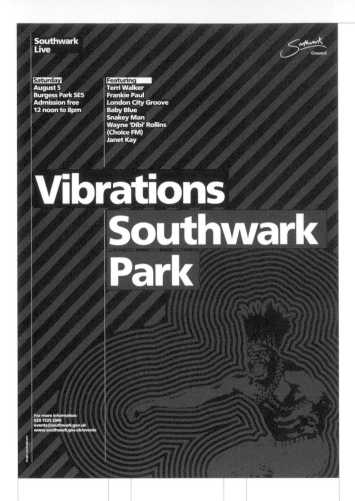

SOUTHWARK LIVE

Design: Tim Sawford at Wire

Southwark Live is one of London's largest events programs.
Wire's brief was to create a functional and flexible visual identity to
convey the vibrancy and diversity of the activities on offer. Designer
Tim Sawford used abstract forms, inspired by the flags often seen
at local events, within a multicolumn and multifield system. Colored
text boxes help to make informational hierarchy clear even against
the more complex photographic images.

I Love Peckham 2006

August 7 to 13
Peckham Town
Centre
Live music, street
performance,
dance, markets,
food and art

August 10
Star Academy

Southwark Live

For more information:
020 7525 2000
events@southwark.gov.uk
www.southwark.gov.uk/events

In association with:

Southwark Live

Saturday
July 3
Southwark Park
SE16
Admission free
1pm to 10pm

Featuring
Joe Brown
Albert Lee and
Hogan's Heroes
The Blockheads

The Event— Southwark Park

For more information:
020 7525 2000
events@southwark.gov.uk
www.scuthwark.gov.uk/events

BBC LONDON
94.9FM

Southwark Council

GRID SPECIFICATIONS

Page size (trimmed)	297 x 420mm
Top margin	10mm
Bottom margin	13.5mm
Outside margin	12mm
Inside margin	8.5mm
Number of columns	16
Gutter width	4mm
Extras	Baseline grid, 0.5mm

MyHome SIEBEN

SEVEN EXPERIMENTS FOR CONTEMPORARY LIVING Interventions by:

EXPERIMENTE FÜR EIN NEUES WOHNEN

Interventionen von:

Jurgen Bey, Ronan & Erwan Bouroullec, Fernando & Humberto Campana, Hella Jongerius, Greg Lynn, Jürgen Mayer H., Jerszy Seymour

AN EXHIBITION AT THE

EINE AUSSTELLUNG IM VITRA DESIGN MUSEUM 14. JUNI – 16. SEPTEMBER 2007

Opening hours		Öffnungszeiten	
Monday–Sunday	10 am–6 pm	Montag–Sonntag	10–18 Uhr
Wednesday	10 am –8 pm	Mittwoch	10–20 Uhr
Guided tours		**Führungen**	
Saturday and Sunday	11 am	Samstag und Sonntag	11 Uhr

Vitra Design Museum
Charles-Eames-Strasse. 1 / D-79576 Weil am Rhein
info-weil@design-museum.de / www.design-museum.de
phone: +49 (0)7921/702 3200
fax +49 (0)7621/702 3590

Vitra Design Museum

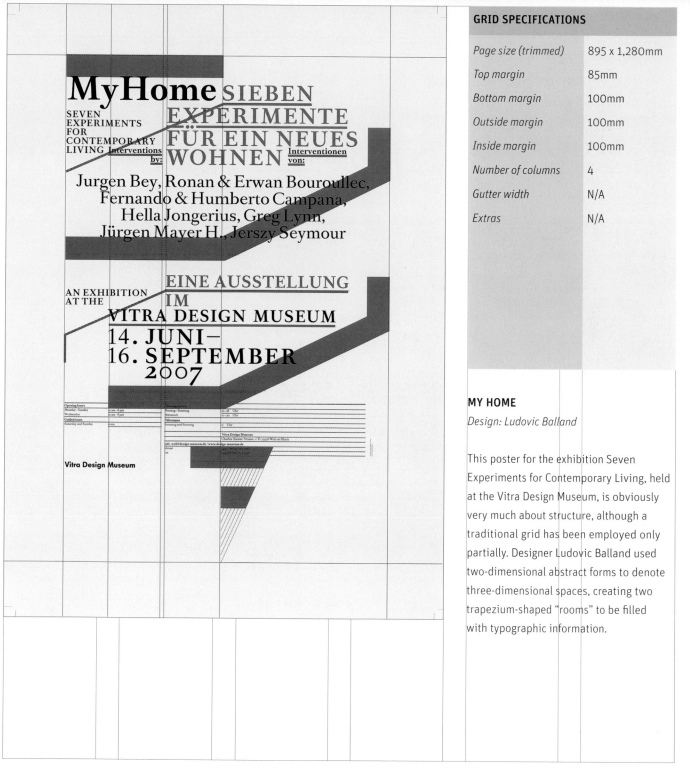

GRID SPECIFICATIONS

Page size (trimmed)	895 x 1,280mm
Top margin	85mm
Bottom margin	100mm
Outside margin	100mm
Inside margin	100mm
Number of columns	4
Gutter width	N/A
Extras	N/A

MY HOME

Design: Ludovic Balland

This poster for the exhibition Seven Experiments for Contemporary Living, held at the Vitra Design Museum, is obviously very much about structure, although a traditional grid has been employed only partially. Designer Ludovic Balland used two-dimensional abstract forms to denote three-dimensional spaces, creating two trapezium-shaped "rooms" to be filled with typographic information.

Index

AA Print Studio **125**
Aarchitecture **125**
Abbeydale **183**
AD (Architectural Design) **167**
Adams, George **197**
Adobe **177, 179, 181**
Airside **190**
alorenz **185**
Ambos, Grégory **125**
America *see* United States
American Modernism: Graphic Design 1920 to 1960 **67**
Amsterdam **137**
angled columns **31**
annual reports **33, 35, 177, 179**
annual reviews **23**
AP Architecture in Practice **95**
APFEL (A Practice for Everyday Life) **165**
architectonics **39**
The Architects' Journal **165**
Architectural Association School of Architecture **125**
art books **137**
Art Institute of California **203**
ASCII **173**

Babyshambles Sessions **205**
Balland, Ludovic **221**
banknotes **169**
bar codes **185**
BaseDESIGN **39, 193**
Bastos, Nuno **51**
Bather, Zoë **25, 147, 153, 155, 183**
Bauhaus **167**
BB/Saunders **99**
Beall, Lester **67**
Berlin **185**
Bittiner, Julian **177, 179**
A Body on the Line **173**
book covers **23, 61**
booklets **47**
Bookman Old Style **95**
books **58–95, 137**
brand images **31, 179**

brochures **20–35, 183**
Brodovitch, Alexey **67**
Building at the Coast **56**
business cards **109**
business-to-business images **31**

calendars **117**
California **31**
captions **61, 67, 79, 121, 159**
Carrot **25**
cartography **147**
catalogs **20–35, 42, 51, 54, 91**
CDs **173, 187**
Chartered Society of Designers **133**
Chartier, Richard **35**
charts **31**
CHK Design **95, 167, 169**
color coding **39**
colored-pencil device **33**
column-and-field grid **56**
comics **61**
concerts **213**
cookery books **83**
corporate review **179**
200% Cotton: New T-Shirt Graphics **73**
300% Cotton: More T-Shirt Graphics **73**
Creative Review **131**
Creative Suite (CS) **181**
Crnokrak, Peter **205, 207**
Croatia Osiguranje **33**
Croatian Architects Association **56**
Croatian National Tourist Board **217**
cross-marks **149**
Crouwel, Wim **42**
Curtis, Matt **159**
cut-outs **121**

Daly, Wayne **125**
Design This Day: 8 Decades of Influential Design **86–87**
Design Typography **23, 25, 61, 67, 133**
The Designer **133**
Device **71, 173**
diagonals **73, 105, 185**
diagrams **25**
diaries **99**
die-cuts **31**

direct mail **31**
DNA Films **190**
Doherty, Pete **205**
Dorfsman, Lou **67**
Douglas, Sarah **165**
downloads **205**
Dumphy, Hannah **169**
Dunraven Secondary School **153**

L'École **25**
eight-column grid **25**
Émigrés **67**
emphasis **42**
EP labels **185**
ephemera **71, 83, 165**
Esterson, Simon **133**
Europe **67, 155**
events page **117**
6=0 exhibition **51**
exhibition design grids **36–57, 91**

FAD **193**
fashion **73, 159**
Fehler **187**
field-based grid **99**
First Congress of Croatian Architects **56**
First Impression **199**
five-column grid **143**
Fl@33 **73, 79**
Fleckhaus, Willy **133**
fliers **188–221**
fluorescent color **31**
folding process **29, 191, 197**
folios **79, 149, 153, 165**
four-column grid **23, 71, 125, 165**
Frutiger, Adrian **203**
Futura **67**

Gale, Nathan **131**
geography **39**
geometry **181, 185, 213**
Gerrit Rietveld Academy **137**
golden section **91, 213**
Gómez, Jason **86**
Grafik **121**
Graham, Ben **86**
graphic guidelines **193**

Graphis **61**
GRAy **137**
Groot, Arjan **47**
Gry, Lane **137**
guidelines **39, 183, 193**

handbooks **95**
hanging heights **54, 105**
Harriman Steel **29, 143, 147, 199**
Harriman-Dickinson, Julian **29, 143, 147, 199**
headlines **95, 159**
Heiman, Eric **91**
Heinisch, Damian **111**
Hidalgo, Reggie **203**
hierarchy of information **33, 218**
highlighting **33, 207**
Hochuli, Jost **67**
Homeosteticos **51**
Horror Vacui: Urban Implosions **47**
Hughes, Rian **71, 173**
Hui-Ling Chen **181**

I Love Távora **211**
identities **39, 73, 96—117, 153, 183, 193, 218**
Ikon Gallery **117**
illustrated books **58—95**
Illustrator CS2 **181**
images **25, 29, 31, 42, 47, 67, 73, 79, 121, 131,
    137, 147, 165, 191, 217**
indents **121, 125**
InDesign **139**
index **61**
Industrial Romantic **71**
inserts **35**
interactivity **139**

Jacquillat, Agathe **73, 79**
Jagdish, Madhavi **91**
Jake Tilson Studio **83**
joinedupdesignforschools **183**
Jorge Jorge Design **105**
journals **99**
Joy Division **209**

kaleidoscopes **185**
Kalmre, Risto **137**
Keith Talent Gallery **169**

King, Laurence **61**
Kitty Cuts **185**
Krah **56**
Küsters, Christian **95, 167, 169**

Lambda Duraflex **205**
landscape images **71**
layering **125**
leading **133**
leaflets **20—35**
lectures **201, 203**
The Libertines **205**
Lightship Visual **201**
limited editions **86**
Lisbon Architecture Triennial **47, 54**
Ljubicic, Boris **33, 56, 215, 217**
logos **95, 167, 183**
London **42, 213, 218**
longitude **147**
lookbooks **29**
loop binding **25**
loose-leaf publications **25**
Lorenz, Angela **185**
Lost Souls **29**
Love Will Tear Us Apart Again **209**
Lund+Slaatto **109**

McNally, Clare **137**
Macs **173**
Madrid **39**
magazines **118—77**
mailers **31, 199**
Malik, Saima **31**
Mamaril, Bryan **86**
manifestos **99, 207**
manuals **137**
MAP **147**
maps **25, 149**
margins **23, 61**
Marten, Karel **23**
mastheads **149**
Matrix **95**
Medley, Stuart **201**
MetaDesign San Francisco **177, 179, 181**
mirroring **31**
Miser & Now **169**
Mission Design **109, 111**

modernists **211**
modular systems **39**
Monographics **61**
mosaics **215**
Mousner, Jim **31**
movie crews **191**
movie stills **61**
Müller, Julia **47**
Müller-Brockmann, Josef **213**
multicolumn grid **53, 61, 73, 99, 121, 131, 155,
    183, 218**
multiculturalism **183**
multipage documents **105**
Murphy, Dom **117**
Museum of Modern Art **39**
My Home **221**

nature **181**
navigation **33, 42, 86, 117, 125, 147, 155,
    197, 203**
needlework **73**
Netherlands **47**
New Caledonia **67**
New Gothic **95**
New York **39**
New Zealand **201**
news-zines **125**
newsletters **118—77**
newspapers **118—77**
Next Level **143, 147**
nine-column grid **42**
Norway **109**
novels **137**
numerals **56**

Old School, New School, TrueType School **201**
On-Site: New Architecture in Spain **39**
On/Off **213**
op art **47**
Origin Design **31**
Otago University **201**
overprinting **23, 199**

± **205, 207, 209**
365 Pages **99**
packaging **173, 178—87**
panels **47, 201**

Pantone **205**

paper stocks **87, 91, 209**

Patterns: New Surface Design **79**

personal project **197**

photography **71, 83, 147, 177, 179, 215**

Pinto, Liliana **54, 211**

pixels **117**

plans **25**

Plastique **159**

Porto **51**

portrait images **71**

Portugal **51, 211**

Portugal, Pedro **53**

postcards **29**

posters **29, 42, 56, 169, 183, 188—221**

print **61, 109, 199**

property brochures **25**

R2 Design **51, 211**

RA Magazine **155**

radiography **181**

Ramalho, Lizá **51, 54, 211**

Rand, Paul **67**

Rebelo, Artur **51, 54, 211**

Reed, Amber **91**

registration **199**

Rossoni, Maggie **203**

Rotary Club **213**

rotated grid **31**

Royal College of Art **213**

Ruder, Emil **201**

rules **165**

running feet **79, 165**

Saetren, Karl Martin **109, 111**

San Diego **31**

Sarson, Richard **213**

Saville, Peter **209**

Sawford, Tim **218**

scale **39, 71, 79, 109, 131**

Scotland **47, 147**

SEA **42, 121**

seminars **213**

Serralves Museum of Contemporary Art **51**

Seven Experiments for Contemporary Living **221**

signage **183**

single-page items **105**

six-column grid **67, 133, 211**

sketchbooks **99**

slanting grid **31**

software **181**

Sorrell Foundation **153, 183**

Southwark Live **218**

space **31, 42, 47, 56, 61, 147, 149, 153**

Spain **39, 193**

Spencer, Herbert **61**

spreads **61**

square format **71**

standfirsts **121, 149**

stationery **105, 109, 111, 183**

Steel, Nick **143, 147**

Stevenson, Freddie **173**

Studio8 Design **153, 155, 159, 183**

Studio International **33, 215, 217**

SUNschrift **23**

Sunshine **190**

supplements **35**

Sutnar, Ladislav **67**

Swiss school **87, 203**

T-Shirt Graphics **73**

tables **31**

tabular matter **33**

tactility **87**

Tak! **117**

A Tale of 12 Kitchens **83**

tartan **47**

Távora, Fernando **211**

Teague **86—87**

technical drafting grid **99**

technical manuals **137**

Ten Proposals **56**

test cards **143**

text **25, 29, 31, 42, 47, 54, 56, 61, 67, 73, 121, 131, 133, 137, 159, 207, 211**

textiles **47**

three dimensions **29, 56, 217, 221**

three-column grid **147**

Tilson, Jake **83**

Time Warner **31**

titles **61, 73, 121**

tourists **217**

tours **39**

Tria markers **205**

Tschichold, Jan **213**

Turnstyle **86—87**

TV color bands **143**

twelve-column grid **79, 87, 159**

two-column grid **147**

type size **133**

Typographica **61**

typography **31, 39, 42, 86, 91, 121, 133, 177, 179, 203, 211**

underlining **33**

Uneasy Nature **91**

United States **35, 67**

United States Green Building Council (USGBC) **35**

urban plans **211**

Urban Voids **54**

Veasey, Nick **181**

vertigo **47**

Vignelli, Massimo **67**

Vitra Design Museum **221**

Vollauschek, Tomi **73, 79**

Volume Inc. **91**

+/VS **187**

Watson, Steve **86**

Weatherspoon Art Museum **91**

websites **99, 117**

Weingart, Wolfgang **201**

Wickens, Brett **177, 181**

Wien (Vienna) **185**

Willey, Matt **147, 153, 155, 159**

Wire **218**

worker/parasite manifesto **207**

X-rays **181**

Yendle, Brad **23, 25, 61, 67, 133**

Zak Group **125**

Zero **153**